Racial Diversity and Social Capital

Race and racial diversity are important aspects of America and have been shown to substantially affect social relations and the political system. At the same time, greater civic association and a general sense of community, which are embodied in the concept of social capital, are said to have tremendous beneficial effects and to profoundly influence American society. This study connects and critically assesses two bodies of research that have come to different conclusions on these issues. Is America's legacy of racial inquality the "evil twin" of the benefits of social capital? When the author analyzes social outcomes for racial minorities in addition to other dimensions of American politics, the impact of racial diversity consistently outweighs that of social capital.

Rodney E. Hero is the Packey J. Dee III Professor of American Democracy in the Department of Political Science at the University of Notre Dame. He is the author of *Latinos and the U.S. Political System* (1992), which received the Ralph J. Bunche Award of the American Political Science Association, and *Faces of Inequality* (1998), winner of the APSA's Woodrow Wilson Foundation Award. Professor Hero is also co-author of *Multi-Ethnic Moments: The Politics of Urban Education Reform* (2006).

Racial Diversity and Social Capital

Equality and Community in America

RODNEY E. HERO

University of Notre Dame

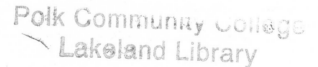

CAMBRIDGE
UNIVERSITY PRESS

CAMBRIDGE UNIVERSITY PRESS
Cambridge, New York, Melbourne, Madrid, Cape Town, Singapore, São Paulo

Cambridge University Press
32 Avenue of the Americas, New York, NY 10013-2473, USA

www.cambridge.org
Information on this title: www.cambridge.org/9780521875516

First published 2007

Printed in the United States of America

A catalog record for this publication is available from the British Library.

Library of Congress Cataloging in Publication Data
Hero, Rodney E., 1953–
Racial diversity and social capital : equality and community in America /
Rodney E. Hero.
p. cm.
Includes bibliographical references and index.
ISBN-13: 978-0-521-87551-6 (hardback)
ISBN-10: 0-521-87551-X (hardback)
ISBN-13: 978-0-521-69861-0 (pbk.)
ISBN-10: 0-521-69861-8 (pbk.)
1. United States – Social conditions – 1980–   2. Pluralism (Social sciences) –
United States.   3. Minorities – United States.   4. Social capital (Sociology) –
United States.   5. Social participation – United States.   6. Equality – United States.
7. Race awareness – United States.   I. Title.
HN59.2.H474   2007
305.800973 – dc22   2006036857

ISBN   978-0521-87551-6 hardback
ISBN   978-0521-69861-0 paperback

to Kathy

Contents

Tables and Figures

TABLES

FIGURES

Preface

In this study I endeavor to shed light on issues that I feel are genuinely significant from the standpoint of (empirical) democratic theory and that also have great normative importance. Essentially, I attempt to reckon with matters of equality, particularly racial (in)equality, as considered and compared through the lenses of two theories that purport to explain some substantial part of equality in America. The *racial diversity* thesis, which focuses on race as tapped by the size of minority populations, and the general sense of "community," as embodied in the concept and as a measure of *social capital*, are used to assess a range of social and political phenomena in the American states

As I try to make clear throughout, the goal is to carefully assess and juxtapose the two theoretical perspectives; it is not to undertake a critique of social capital as such. Readers may nonetheless view this book as (primarily) a critique of social capital, but that would be a misreading of this effort. Critiques tend to be thought of as a kind of "looking back at" and retrospective analysis of scholarly theories and assertions, as reactions against or responses to previously existing arguments. In the process of systematically considering analytical perspectives, some element of a critique of social capital is implicit and perhaps inevitable, but that is not the main thrust of my efforts. When examining the racial diversity and social capital theses we should bear in mind that the former preceded the latter (Hero 1992; Hero and Tolbert 1996; Hero 1998), certainly as the social capital thesis was fully elaborated in the case of American politics (see Putnam 2000). Social capital research overlooked racial diversity in general and did not acknowledge specific renderings of the racial diversity thesis. In important respects, "which came first" – and whether Putnam's *Bowling Alone* ignored the racial diversity thesis – is beside the point.

What *is* crucial is what the two analytical perspectives can tell us about fundamental political questions. As will be seen, I suggest that race and community are interrelated and interact to some extent; thus the two theories have some overlap. But I also stress they are decidedly different interpretations. I find that a sense of community (as summarized in the social capital index; Putnam 2000) is not generally associated with greater relative racial equality and, indeed, may occasionally be linked to worse outcomes. Additionally, its ability to explain other political phenomena is much more limited than one might expect in light of the claims of social capital theorists. On the other hand, racial diversity is shown to have consistent and substantial impacts.

Social theories should be judged not by their origins or traditions, or by how intuitively appealing they seem, but rather by what they actually achieve in their range and depth of explanatory capacity; they should be examined and evaluated on the basis of their substantive merits. Similarly, theories should be assessed not only by their accuracy but also by their adequacy and appropriateness – that is, not only by whether they are "correct" but also by how complete and how well they address the specific issues in question.

Leading interpretations have been shown to be limited in their capacity to address the racial dimensions that have been a major and enduring feature of American politics. Pluralism was questioned on the basis of its class biases; as Schattschneider (1960) famously remarked, "the flaw in the pluralist heaven is that the heavenly chorus sings with a strong upper class accent" (see also

Stone 1980). And later scholarship directly demonstrated pluralism's shortcomings regarding race and minority groups' voices, delineating the concept of "two-tiered pluralism" by explaining the essentially structural nature of racial politics and how standard pluralism was in fact even more racially contingent than had previously been recognized (Hero 1992). Another highly influential theory of American state politics, "political culture" (Elazar 1972, 1984), was examined relative to racial and white ethnic diversity and was shown to be substantially an artifact of such diversity (Hero 1998). In this book I develop and apply arguments that are directly informed by the two-tiered pluralism thesis and that also parallel (but go well beyond) previous considerations of political culture and racial diversity. These arguments are then juxtaposed to those of social capital theorists.

Pluralism is an *interest*-based argument, whereas social capital and political culture arguments emphasize largely nonmaterial *ideas* about social networks and interactions. These concern the levels of trust and civic association (social capital) and the orientation and prevalence of certain substantive ideas (political culture) in polities. Pluralism's emphasis on group activities – and social capital's emphasis on civic association and cooperation – appears to understate social structure and formal *institutions* of politics in different ways and to different degrees, which seems especially consequential for how issues of race are approached and the conclusions ultimately drawn. In contrast, diversity arguments contend that the racial dimensions of American politics *include* structural and institutional elements along with interests and ideas (Hero 1992, ch. 10; Hero 1998, ch. 8; Clarke et al. 2006; King and Smith 2005). Additionally, the racial diversity thesis brings attention to ideas not emphasized in social capital studies and links those ideas to racial dimensions of American belief systems.

Ultimately, this book argues that racial diversity continues to shape American politics, including its civic inclinations, in ways that often perpetuate negative social and political patterns as well as racial inequality. In some circumstances the size of minority populations may mitigate but not entirely neutralize the extent of minority inequality. Racial diversity generally surpasses social capital as a discernible influence in several arenas of American politics. Moreover, I show that social capital falls well short of prior claims about its salutary benefits for equality, especially racial equality. Instead, social capital in the aggregate has few beneficial (and some detrimental) consequences for relative racial equality.

Despite these remarks (which are further developed in the book), I must also say something that may sound peculiar: I do wish that the social capital thesis were true and broadly applicable in its suggestion that higher social capital leads to greater equality and, by extension, to greater racial equality. The corollary is that I wish the racial diversity thesis were (empirically) false – that racial diversity no longer explained important social outcomes, political processes, or policies. In short, I would be delighted if the theory I advance were wrong, because the implications of my being wrong would be outcomes that are patently desirable from a normative standpoint. However, the evidence in this book strongly suggests otherwise. The weight of the evidence falls heavily in support of the racial diversity thesis and decidedly against the social capital thesis.

Comprehending how race has shaped and continues to shape sense of community, and vice versa, warrants considerable intellectual attention as well as appropriate civic practices and public policies. I therefore conclude that our time and efforts as scholars, and as a society, are more fruitfully directed at understanding community and inequality from a racial perspective than from emphasizing other perspectives that are inattentive to race.

I should offer a brief note about certain words and concepts. The reader will see that I use the word(s) "racial," "ethnic," "minorities," and "racial/ethnic" frequently in the book. For present purposes, I use these words essentially interchangeably; at the same time I fully recognize, of course, that each concept may have different meanings to different people in social relations and public discourse – as well as in analyses undertaken by scholars within and across scholarly disciplines. There are somewhat different understandings and often contentiousness about the meaning(s) and application(s) of the words. I acknowledge that complexity by using the various terms as they seem most appropriate and clear in specific instances, though I can hardly begin to address (much less settle) the issues connected with the various understandings. Instead, I sometimes use the terms separately (though their meanings may overlap) and sometimes use them together. That said, the group most commonly and directly considered in assessing the many questions addressed is blacks/African Americans, although Hispanics/Latinos are also discussed on several occasions.

Acknowledgments

A large number of friends, family, colleagues, and fellow scholars have played significant roles in the development of this book, and many of them in more than one way. I appreciate all their encouragement, inspiration, and good will – more than I can say.

Caroline J. Tolbert, a co-author with me on various papers on the racial diversity thesis, co-authored Chapter 5 of this book; she also provided many useful comments and suggestions on several parts of the project. Rob Preuhs contributed a great deal through his thoughtful comments on a range of ideas concerning the topics covered here and a host of related issues; he also provided data analysis and collection that strengthened the book's empirical base.

I have also learned much from conversations with Ken Meier, Rene Rocha, and Dan Hawes as well as from their research on racial diversity and social capital, part of which is drawn on directly in this book. I have likewise gained important insights on the topics from discussions with and research of Eric Uslaner and Kim Hill.

I appreciate the comments and observations of those who attended a presentation (in April 2002) at the Center for American Political Studies (CAPS) in Harvard's Department of Government; they include Theda Skocpol, Robert Putnam, Jennifer

Hochschild, and Sidney Verba. The paper I presented there was one of my early analyses of racial diversity and its relationship to social capital.

The University of Notre Dame has been most generous in supporting all my scholarly and teaching endeavors. I am thankful to all my colleagues in the Department of Political Science there. Those whose interest and ideas most directly intersect with the subject of this book, and with whom I discussed it and from whom I benefited, are Al Tillery, John Griffin, Ben Radcliff, and Tony Messina. Some all-too-brief conversations with sociologist Robert Fishman also helped. The resources provided by the Packey J. Dee III Professorship in American Democracy have fostered my scholarly efforts immensely over the last five years. Considerable support from the Institute for Latino Studies was also helpful.

I'm especially grateful to Susan Clarke and to Larry Dodd for strongly urging me to pursue this project, as well as for their friendship, advice, and wisdom over many years. Mara Sidney has been similarly supportive.

I have also been stimulated by and have learned a great deal from my collaborators on other projects. In addition to a number of those previously mentioned, Luis Fraga, John Garcia, Michael Jones-Correa, Valerie Martinez-Ebers, and Gary Segura – my co-investigators on the Latino National Survey (LNS) – have become close scholarly companions and friends.

I also express deep gratitude to social sciences editor Eric Crahan at Cambridge University Press for his support and guidance as well as to copy editor Matt Darnell for his wonderfully careful and thorough work on the manuscript.

Finally, I express my deepest gratitude and appreciation to those who are closest to me: my wife, Kathy, my daughter, Lindsay, and my step-children, Chris and Jen, as well as my mother, father, and sister. I'm so very fortunate, and most thankful, for the inspiration they provide.

Introduction

Has America's sense of "community" been racially constrained and contingent? In other words, has American civil society, politics, and a broader collective sense of self been shaped about as much by racial and ethnic differentiation (i.e., racial/ethnic "diversity") as by more general and supposedly inclusive conceptions of social connectedness and commonwealth, civic republicanism, or "social capital"? Do America's practices – and perhaps very understanding – of community continue to be shaped in substantial part by racial factors, even though forty years have passed since civil rights legislation was enacted? Do understandings of race affect perceptions of what are considered to be appropriate and actual community bounds, and do notions of community define and/or reinforce racial/ethnic differentiation? Beyond formal citizenship and legal guarantees of civil rights, what criteria implicitly (or explicitly) define the depth and breadth of "who really belongs"? Are the two sets of social phenomena – race and community – normatively (and actually) antithetical, symbiotic, intertwined, or related in other ways? Has scholarly research effectively acknowledged these possibilities and analyzed them accordingly? These complex and difficult questions motivate the present study.

The issues examined here certainly speak to these questions, although it is unlikely that any single study can satisfactorily grapple with the many dimensions identified. Therefore, this inquiry is somewhat more focused and asks: Has the reality been one of a civil society and a polity that is racially constrained and conditional (Hero 1998; cf. Orr 1999)? In other words, is the social capital interpretation (Putnam 2000) a reasonable and accurate – or rather an incomplete and romanticized – depiction of American community? How should we study the American polity when addressing such questions? What is the appropriate type of evidence to consider, and what do we learn in the view of one analytical approach versus another?

These complicated issues have been implied but only tentatively probed in the political science research literature, and these social forces have not been systematically examined jointly in contemporary political science empirical analysis. There have been numerous commentaries as well as a number of critiques of social capital, including the application of the thesis to the United States. Yet the present study is unique in systematically examining the social capital argument through the lens of an alternative theoretical perspective: racial diversity. The large bodies of empirical research on social capital ("community") and on racial/ethnic diversity offer dramatically different portrayals of the American political system; examining them together may offer a way of better attending to pressing questions. However, these bodies of research have, with few exceptions, developed along separate paths and with little cross-examination, intersection, or integration. Perhaps this is understandable given that contemporary political science is commonly segmented by subfield specialization and differing methodological approaches; the disconnectedness may also be due to the different world views of scholars. The implication by social capital studies (e.g., Putnam 2000) of something like an era of a civic "American Dream" should be kept in perspective by the historic and continuing "American Dilemma" of race (Myrdal 1944; DuBois 1935).

Particularly striking is that – despite largely overlooking issues of race, including a substantial body of research that has documented its role – the social capital interpretation continues to hold sway over scholars of American politics (Putnam 2000; Gray 1999, 1996). (More recent research on social capital has begun to engage issues of race and immigration, however.) Whatever the reasons for the separation of the two approaches and for the frequent neglect of racial aspects of American community by the social capital thesis, one consequence has been to forestall a broader and better understanding. A principal aim of the current study is to connect and critically assess these two bodies of research – an especially compelling goal in that the United States has never simultaneously had high formal racial/ethnic equality (much less substantive equality) *and* high social capital: the decline of social capital (as documented in Putnam 2000) coincided with the emergence of formal racial equality. As racial/ethnic complexity evolves with an increasingly multiethnic population (Clarke et al. 2006) and with the large immigration in the 1980s and 1990s, the relevance of these issues continues and in some ways increases.

A core goal of this book is to examine jointly the analytical perspectives of research on racial diversity and social capital in order to juxtapose and thereby assess how and why they differ as well as how much they inform our understanding of recent and contemporary American politics. I shall assess the accuracy and (perhaps more importantly) the adequacy and appropriateness of theoretical perspectives as vantage points for comprehending American politics. In exploring these two perspectives I engage an intriguing and important puzzle in American politics. Previous research indicates that *higher racial diversity* is associated with lesser and *less equitable political processes* and public policy outcomes (even after accounting for a host of other factors; see Hero 1998). At the same time, *higher levels of social capital* are consistently associated with *better processes and outcomes* (Putnam 2000). Can both arguments be equally correct? Does one set of claims sufficiently take into account the other?

If conditions are indeed better in high social capital settings, for whom are they better? Are conditions better for essentially all – that is, for a majority in absolute/aggregate terms, or for some groups more than others? And should overall or instead relative evaluative standards be used in making such judgments? Finally, are the evaluative criteria applied and the indicators used to assess evidence themselves associated with a particular analytical perspective? Depending on the answers to these questions, diversity's importance may be emphasized more or less, so at times social capital arguments may be interpreted as mistaking a problem for a solution.

Although overlooked in much of the early social capital research designs, racial diversity and social capital in the American states may be related (Hero 2003a,b, 1998). Empirical analysis shows that states with high social capital tend to be racially homogeneous (white), whereas states with high racial/ethnic diversity tend to have low levels of social capital (Hero 2003a; cf. Putnam 2000). Is this correlation a coincidence or is there an underlying connection (causal mechanism) between the two? Is America's legacy of racial inequality the "evil twin" of its social capital? Are they, at least to some extent, two sides of the same coin – a kind of yin and yang flowing together, each containing the seed of the other in U.S. politics? There is reason to believe they could well be related in these ways (Smith 1993; King and Smith 2005). It is widely agreed that race has been a weighty factor in American political and social history (see, e.g., Key 1949; DuBois 1935), but there is debate concerning precisely how *much* weight compared with such other social factors as social class, formal and informal institutions, and sense of community (Hero and Radcliff 2005). This study will pursue and, it is hoped, illuminate these questions with respect to race and social capital.

THE SOCIAL AND THEORETICAL LANDSCAPE

The United States has been among the most racially and ethnically diverse of the Western democracies, and demographic complexity and change have been central traits of its politics (Key 1949; Hero 1998). Most of the thinking on and analysis of race in America has, understandably, been in terms of white and black politics; that orientation has substantially influenced social capital analyses and racial diversity studies as well. According to the 2000 census, whites (non-Hispanic) constitute 71 percent of the population and Latinos over 13 percent. African Americans account for roughly 12 percent of the population and Asians 4–5 percent. Contrast this with 1980, when 79 percent of the U.S. population was white, 12 percent African American, 6.4 percent Latino, and 1.6 percent Asian American. By 2005, four American states – including the two most populous, California and Texas – had become "majority minority" states, with Latinos as the largest component; altogether, nine U.S. states had minority populations of 40 percent or more. The U.S. Census Bureau projects that, by the year 2025, whites will account for 61 percent of the population, Latinos 18 percent, African Americans 14 percent and Asian Americans almost 7 percent. Hence, by this estimate, in slightly over 40 years the white population will decrease by about 20 percent to little more than 60 percent of the population. Demographic forces and demographic diversity continue to alter the face of the American polity, yet the implications for social capital's evolution and relevance have not yet been fully addressed, and the diversity thesis has only begun to incorporate these changes into its theorizing (but see, Hero 1992; Hero and Preuhs 2006; Clarke et al. 2006; Fraga et al. 2006). Most of the empirical analysis in this study that directly compares racial groups draws on evidence of black versus white differences; however, specific attention is also given to Latinos in several instances (e.g., see Hawes, Rocha, and Meier's 2006 analysis in Chapter 4 and the latter parts of Chapter 5).

A number of scholarly studies were published from the mid-1990s onward documenting, despairing of, and seeking to explain a steep decline in "civic community," "civic engagement," and "social capital" in the United States that was associated with decreasing political participation and diminished democracy (Putnam 2000; cf. Skocpol 2003). It is probably no coincidence that these studies were written while demographic, social, and public policy changes emerged in legislation of the 1960s and were amplified in the early 1990s. These developments – declining social capital and (increased) racial diversity – have been seen as largely unrelated and distinct in practice; moreover, scholarly research on social capital has asserted that racial diversity and the decline of social capital are not connected (Putnam 2000; Skocpol 2003). The initial signs of the decline of social capital became evident in the mid-1960s (Putnam 2000), which happened to coincide with the adoption of such policies for formal equality as the Civil Rights Act (1964), the Voting Rights Act (1965), immigration (1965) and open housing (1968) legislation, as well as other developments, including urban riots, with implications for racial issues. Yet the leading study of social capital and politics has argued emphatically that the changed legal situation of blacks and other minorities, and racial diversity and change more generally, were *not* associated with the decline of social capital (Putnam 2000). Nonetheless, this coincidence is certainly intriguing and worthy of careful analysis (but is not a core issue animating this study and is thus only briefly engaged in later discussion).

This book offers a wide-ranging treatment of the puzzle regarding racial diversity versus and/or in relation to social capital as manifested in American politics. I first review, summarize, and mull over racial diversity and social capital as theories in order to better understand their claims and their strengths and weaknesses; in the process, the philosophical and associated normative underpinnings of the theories are considered. I explore the explanatory power of each theory, individually and comparatively, and to some extent consider their interactions – juxtaposing the underlying assumptions, research approaches, and claims of theories emphasizing racial/ethnic factors on the one hand, and "community" on the other hand, for social and political equality. The basic claims and supporting evidence of the social capital thesis are delineated; similarly, the arguments and studies supporting the diversity interpretation are presented. Several analyses that draw on state-level data and on national opinion data are presented. This approach permits consideration of the two sets of propositions in a more directly comparative fashion and allows a comprehensive and careful treatment of the relative influence of racial diversity and social capital on social outcomes, civic and economic equality, aggregate and individual participation, and policy outputs in America, specifically, the American *states*.

A BROADER CONTEXT: A MULTIPLE TRADITIONS APPROACH

Before summarizing the analysis to be presented in later chapters, I think it useful to discuss scholarship that provides an intellectual backdrop for the current study. The significance of multiple theoretical or philosophical traditions in American politics – including the importance of aspects of American society associated with the "ascriptive hierarchy" or "inegalitarian" tradition – has been increasingly acknowledged (Smith 1993, 1997; King and Smith 2005). Those inegalitarian orientations are relevant for gender, economic, and racial inequality and other social dimensions. A varied literature has emphasized the connections between such inequalities (see, e.g., Strolovitch 2007; Hochschild 1995; Hero and Radcliff 2005), though many studies have tended to focus on one or the other.

Scholarship has increasingly stressed the multiple traditions as central to a fuller understanding of politics in the American states (Hero 1998; cf. Elazar 1966, 1972, 1984; Thompson, Ellis, and Wildavsky 1990). These concerns have been commonly recognized at a general level, particularly in works of normative political theory. However, *empirical democratic theory* research on social and policy outcomes in American politics has rather seldom followed suit; on the whole, such research focused on the macro level has neither adequately incorporated the multiple traditions perspective in a systematic manner nor compared the multiple traditions as alternative (or complementary) explanations of important political and policy phenomena. There has certainly been a vast literature in political psychology on *individuals'* attitudes and beliefs about race and race-based versus race-neutral public policies, engaging such matters as "symbolic racism," "social dominance" and other analytical viewpoints (see, e.g., Sears et al. 2000; see also Chapter 7). But those micro-level studies do not examine aggregate social outcomes, actual policy formulation and implementation, or their effects on various racial groups; nor have they considered political participation and various other issues most relevant to the present study (cf. Hero 1998, 2003a,b).

Rogers Smith's treatment (1993, 1997) is frequently viewed as the most explicit and perhaps one of the earliest statements of the "multiple traditions" thesis (but see Stevens 1995). Focusing on writers who analyze the American ("national") political tradition, Smith emphasizes there are three major strands. These include not only *liberal* (or liberty, "individualism," etc.) and *republican* (or civic republicanism or "community" and "fraternity") ideas, as is commonly recognized, but also *ascriptive inegalitarianism*, which was most relevant to providing "justifications" for racial, gender, and class inequality (Smith 1997; cf. Elazar 1966; Putnam 2000, p. 355). One of Smith's central assertions is that much American politics literature and research stresses the former two traditions while neglecting or understating the third.

Smith demonstrates how public discourse and practices in American politics have actually interwoven the three traditions, including ascriptive inegalitarianism, but he also emphasizes that many theorists – including such major writers as Tocqueville, Myrdal, and Hartz – have not adequately recognized this in their work. Much empirical research in American politics is similarly limited in not adequately considering the impact of ascriptve inegalitarianism as it echoes in contemporary racial differentiation.

Examining states' politics through "racial diversity" (as I do here) is emblematic of a multiple traditions perspective, but it also makes several important theoretical and empirical advances. The thesis makes direct links between the theoretical traditions and racial contexts, systematically arguing that such contexts (more or less racially diverse) are more or less strongly associated with manifestations of ascriptive inegalitarianism – and even with civic republicanism and, in turn, with different "faces" of racial inequality (Hero 1998, ch. 1). Although numerous other studies, including Key's (1949) seminal work, have emphasized the importance of race in American politics, the diversity thesis as such (Hero and Tolbert 1996; Hero 1998) differs in some important ways. Unlike other race-focused studies, the diversity thesis posits race as a *generally* important and pervasive social force that is germane to all states and localities, including those that are relatively homogeneous; it also highlights the importance of examining relative social outcomes by race (Soss et al. 2001; Hill 1994; Giles and Hertz 1994; cf. Meier, Stewart, and England 1989; Johnson 2001; Hero and Tolbert 1996; Hero 1998). Furthermore, racial diversity has been explored with respect to a wider range of issues than most race studies, including the impact of race on political and governmental institutions and processes (see Hero 1998 and Chapter 3).

With its claims about social capital and emphasizing a "community" (versus individualist) social and political orientation, Putnam's *Bowling Alone* (*BA*) is solidly rooted in the civic republican tradition. At the same time, the social capital thesis (Putnam 2000, cf. Rice and Sumberg 1997) appears to be a clear example of the tendency of civic republican accounts of American politics generally to understate the legacy of the racial or ascriptive hierarchy tradition, as Smith argues (Smith 1993, pp. 551–2, 557; cf. Hero 1998; pp. 9–23, 32–5; Thompson et al. 1990, ch. 13). Other, broadly similar works, including the "political culture" arguments discussed later (see Elazar 1972, 1984; Lieske 1993; cf. Rice and Sumberg 1997, Fitzpatrick and Hero 1988) similarly do not give race adequate attention in discussing the "traditionalistic," hierarchical culture, much less the "commonwealth" or moralist orientation (Hero 1998; see Chapters 2 and 3 herein). In so emphasizing community and consensus, equality is a secondary concern that is presumed to be an almost natural by-product of high social capital; invidious social differentiation is overlooked or assumed to be mitigated in civic republican renderings of American politics.

Woven into the current study is a consideration of how the several philosophical traditions have been evident in the practices and empirical studies of American politics. Each tradition – and its associated body of empirical research – brings somewhat different conceptual, methodological, and normative lenses that bear, if only implicitly, on *what* is studied and on *how* it is studied. I examine two traditions in terms of their particular implications for policy, participation, and racial inequality dilemmas in American society; the economic class aspects of inegalitarianism are also considered via control variables in several dimension of the empirical analysis that follow in Chapters 4–6. I consider the relevance of the major traditions, particularly the two with a more explicitly collective focus – racial diversity (which draws out the implications and legacy of the ascriptive inegalitarian tradition) and social capital (civic republicanism) – for various indicators that address racial aspects of political equality in the American states. The liberal tradition is not directly examined, in part because of its more individualist nature, although the importance of certain liberal principles for various aspects of equality is considered. Given liberalism's place as the dominant political tradition and as a benchmark for the other two traditions, its impact is surely pervasive although difficult to operationalize and hence to examine effectively for present purposes. However, to the extent that some aspects of liberal and conservative ideas have been explored in studies that parallel this one, those ideas seem to have little relevance for issues of relative racial inequality (Hero 2003b). The evidence presented in subsequent chapters suggests that research rooted in traditions that emphasize community tend *not* to be systematically attentive to the legacy of hierarchy, including its racial elements, and therefore produce analysis and conclusions that have blind spots – one might say color-blind spots – in theoretically limiting and problematic ways (cf. Smith 1993; Hero 2003b).

A great deal of scholarship has in different ways and to different degrees suggested (though seldom explicitly elaborated upon) multiple perspectives in its theorizing and analyses of American politics. But a more developed application is warranted for several reasons, and I will endeavor to provide one here. One reason to do so is that previous work has addressed these issues only briefly, partially, and often indirectly (Elazar 1966, 1984; see also Hero 1998; Hill 1994). A more direct approach can broaden the discussion and better link it to general work on American – as well as comparative – politics, civic culture, public policy, and social well-being (Putnam 1993, 1995, 2000; Skocpol, Ganz, and Munson 2000; Rice and Sumberg 1997; Hero 1998). Another reason to conceive of the research as being associated with several traditions is that most previous studies have examined social or policy outcomes as the dependent variables and do not directly address evidence that considers different traditions, particularly outcomes that might reveal the implications of race. Thus, a more complex, complete, and substantively different picture of American politics may emerge when viewed in the way proposed here.

As with a number of recent studies of diversity and of social capital, the focus here is on the states (Putnam 2000; Rice and Sumberg 1997; Knack 2002), which is appropriate because the states are the primary makers of domestic policy in the American federal system. This federal system is itself a synthesis of two intellectual traditions. The relationship between the national ("federal") government and the states, often referred to as a "commercial republic," implies national government authority over commerce, especially "interstate commerce" and other powers of the federal government delineated in Article I,

section 8, of the U.S. Constitution. (These broadly corre-
spond to "liberalism," including economic liberalism or liberal
capitalism.) The second tradition suggests civic republican or
civic virtue ideas, implying (among other things) the rights of
states to establish and maintain "moral order" within their
boundaries (Elazar 1984). Hence the "police powers" have traditionally been most strongly associated with state governments'
authority concerning the "health, safety, morals, and well-being"
of their citizens. This implies that states hold major authority for
a host of fundamental social policy concerns, as evident in the
profound importance of the concept of "states' rights" in shaping American politics, including its racial order.

Hence racial diversity scholarship has commonly recognized
and followed the exhortation that multiple traditions need to
be taken seriously in studies of American politics (Smith 1993,
1997; Hero 1998; King and Smith 2005). At the same time,
diversity studies especially emphasize that ascriptive hierarchy –
in particular, its ethnic dimensions – has not been adequately
acknowledged or incorporated into theory and research in American politics, and they stress the importance of doing so. The
racial diversity thesis underscores the importance of recognizing
racial/ethnic contexts and the different facets and effects of race
in American politics, not simply collective or aggregate "levels"
or factors that, like social capital studies, implicitly overlook
differentiation (Smith 1993; Hero 1998, pp. 17–23, 140–4; cf.
Putnam 2000; Erikson, Wright, and McIver 1993).

In short, a number of major theoretical and empirical studies,
dating from the 1960s and up to the present, can be situated relative to one (or more) philosophical traditions in American politics. However insightful, many of these studies have on the whole
understated the significance of race, and of racial context and the
distributional aspects of politics. They have not recognized that
racial configurations and that who *else* (i.e., what other groups)
are part of the community and polity could well be relevant to
the very formation and sustenance of social capital and a variety
of civic and political issues (Hero 1998). Social capital studies'

research designs are similarly limited in their ability to assess relative racial outcomes of this "other America," although they consider issues of class (in)equality somewhat directly.

Other studies seemingly make arguments that at least implicitly complement those developed here. The theme of one study concerning race and politics, "Language Policy and Identity Politics in the United States" (Schmidt 2000), is that the two major contesting views on language policy are rooted in concern for "the common good" on the one hand and for "justice" or "equality" on the other, broadly paralleling the civic republican and racial diversity orientations, respectively. Additionally, in a study of American mass attitudes about social welfare policy, Feldman and Steenbergen (2001) develop a distinction between "humanitarian" and "egalitarian" orientations. They argue that humanitarianism, defined as "a sense of responsibility for one's fellow human beings that translates into a belief that one would help" those in need, was recognized as far back as Tocqueville's time and is also associated with one's having a "pro-social orientation." They cite others who ascribe the "high levels of *civic volunteerism* in the United States to humanitarianism" (Feldman and Steenbergen 2001, p. 660, emphasis added). Note that civic volunteerism is a central component of the concept and the operationalization of social capital (Putnam 1993, 2000; Skocpol et al. 2000). "Egalitarianism is associated with support for an active government that routinely intervenes in a number of economic processes" (Feldman and Steenbergen 2001, p. 659; cf. Erikson et al. 1993). Although we cannot pursue these issues further here, I would simply suggest – and believe Feldman and Steenbergen imply as well – that humanitarianism is linked to the civic republican tradition while egalitarianism is linked to the liberal tradition as understood in contemporary America and in the contradictions suggested by racial inequality (and partly manifested in notion of racial diversity). However, since the issue is not central to their study, it is not clear whether the humanitarian (civic republican) or the egalitarian (liberal) concepts are directly attentive specifically to issues of ascriptive inegalitarianism and racial equality in the Feldman and Steenbergen analysis. (I will have occasion to suggest how competing perspectives on individual or micro-level research on attitudes about race-based policies echo the differences of racial diversity and social capital views.)

In summary, many works in American politics are grounded in multiple traditions – though often indirectly or unconsciously – yet they seldom emphasize more than one of the traditions (the clearest exceptions are Smith 1993 and Hero 1998, 2003a,b). It also seems that the orientation most often overlooked is that of ascriptive inegalitarianism and racial hierarchy. But that tradition has been an important element in American political and social history. Moreover, as I shall demonstrate, the other traditions that have heavily shaped American politics research – civic republicanism and liberalism – do not (alone or jointly) account for a number of inequalities in American state politics and policy, or they are related to those policies in ways that actually contradict their own arguments (see Hero 2003b).

OVERVIEW

This introduction has identified and briefly summarized the basic questions and issues to be addressed in the book – that is, the different understandings, findings, and interpretations of American politics represented by the racial diversity perspective on politics (specifically, as developed by Hero and Tolbert 1996 and Hero 1998) and the contemporary social capital thesis (as developed in political science by Putnam 2000). Again, the two interpretations offer dramatically different pictures of American politics; they are also part of a larger discourse linked to American philosophical traditions as evidenced in empirical political science research at the macro level, as emphasized here, and also at the micro level (which is occasionally noted in the present study). What do we find when we juxtapose the two arguments? In attempting to answer this broader question, two related questions are considered, with the first receiving more attention than the second in the subsequent analyses. Does one theory consistently explain more than the other regarding social and political outcomes in the United States; and, after race is appropriately accounted for, does social capital really explain as much as has been claimed? Second, how do notions of race and community interact to affect social outcomes and political participation? In attempting to make sense of, evaluate, and draw conclusions about the impacts of diversity and community – and the corresponding empirical research – the book proceeds as follows.

Chapter 2, "The Social Capital Thesis," provides an extensive summary of the argument, evidence, and conclusions of Putnam (2000). It also discusses other studies in the social capital tradition that focus on other dimensions of government, politics, and public policy (these include studies by Knack 2002; Rice and Sumberg 1997; Elazar 1972, 1984; and Hill and Matsubayashi 2005). The chapter illustrates the relatively long lineage of empirical analyses that set out these arguments; it also notes some theoretical and conceptual limitations. Furthermore, the chapter delineates and discusses the close connection of social capital to an earlier "political culture" thesis that had been examined through a racial diversity lens (Hero 1988).

Chapter 3, "The Racial Diversity Thesis," provides a summary of the argument, evidence, and conclusions of the racial diversity thesis (as developed by Hero and Tolbert 1996 and Hero 1998); additionally, various other studies broadly similar to and compatible with racial diversity arguments are summarized and the implications of their findings discussed. Chapters 4–6 include systematic evaluations, with considerable empirical analysis, of the racial diversity and social capital theses jointly, in particular with regard to questions of racial diversity and equality. The evidence strongly challenges essentially all of the major claims of the social capital thesis.

Chapter 4 considers "Substantive Policy Outcomes and Economic and Civic Equality," examining empirical evidence that served as the primary bases for claims about the salutary effects of social capital for numerous social outcomes (Putnam 2000, chs. 16–22). The evidence provided in the current analysis finds that the outcomes *for minorities* in high – social capital states are no better than in other settings (and are often worse), severely undermining social capital claims. And this is so whether we consider social outcomes in terms of black/white ratios (i.e., *within* states) or black rates *across* states. The beneficial impacts of social capital identified in previous research are the result of the situation for whites, not blacks; a higher level of aggregate social capital (and higher for whites) does not seem to interact with race in a way that elevates the situation of minorities. Thus we can legitimately ask: better *for whom?* – and the answer is not compatible with social capital's assertions (Putnam 2000; Hero 2003a). Similarly, we challenge social capital's suggestion that one form of inegalitarianism – economic inequality – is diminished, at least in the case of blacks.

Chapter 5 examines the impact of racial diversity and social capital on aggregate voter turnout in American elections, considering the direct, the conditional, or the interactive effects on political participation over time; it also examines individual participation in the broader contexts of race and social capital. According to previous research, higher levels of social capital are associated with higher participation, and higher levels of racial diversity are associated with lower participation. Here, state racial diversity is found to have direct, indirect, and conditional effects on voter turnout rates; so does social capital. Hence, both race and social capital matter substantially for this particular aspect of American politics, and their interaction is intriguing. I also examine whether individuals residing in states with higher racial diversity have a decreased probability of voting and other forms of political participation (attending rallies, volunteering for a political party, displaying a bumper sticker) while controlling for other factors. That is, we ask whether respondents in states with higher social capital are more likely to vote and engage in other forms of political participation; they are not. This chapter offers some support for the social capital argument, but diversity seems to explain at least as much and probably more. However, there are interesting interactive effects of the two on voter participation.

Chapter 6 brings in issues that have not generally been addressed in social capital, or in much racial diversity research: public policy *outputs*. After making the case for the appropriateness and importance of considering these issues to begin with, several policies are explored. As much as one can tell from the admittedly tentative evidence, racial diversity does seem to be related to some of the policies; on the other hand, social capital appears to have limited impact on the outputs studied. Overall, the findings are more suggestive than definitive.

Finally, I conclude by weighing and reflecting upon the scholarship and arguments developed in the preceding chapters. In sum, when racial diversity is appropriately factored in to the research design and political and policy indicators (Hero 1998), the salutary effects of aggregate social capital are dramatically diminished, and it is suggested that those effects may in (large) part be an artifact of racial diversity; diversity usually appears to be more important than social capital. The shortcomings of the social capital thesis in incorporating the importance of race as a critical (and constraining) factor in American civil society render it fundamentally more limited than has been recognized. Hence this thesis leads to conclusions that are questionable and arguably misleading and may frequently be just wrong.

I arrive at these conclusions after considering an array of evidence, primarily macro- but also some micro-level, apposite to a range of theoretical and empirical issues raised by the racial diversity and social capital arguments. This enables a reasonably broad and systematic basis to examine and juxtapose and so consider the interactions of these two influential interpretations of (contemporary) American politics – especially their implications for matters of racial/ethnic equality and national community. The theorizing and associated evidence that is grounded in the racial diversity thesis and marshaled here shows that notions of "community" in the United State have been and (empirically) remain racially contingent and interconnected. Social capital arguments have obscured this in not adequately comprehending and confronting these implications. It is quite likely that a sense of community, along with other dimensions of American politics, continues to have a racially two-tiered quality (Hero 1992). The findings in this book are individually and collectively more supportive of a racial diversity interpretation and cast serious doubt on the social capital thesis.

That this sense of community (at least in the United States) has indeed been much less racially egalitarian than implied by the social capital thesis raises doubts also about whether a revival of social capital, at least as understood and recommended by some of the leading theorists of that perspective (Putnam 2000), would actually lead to the ostensibly desired results. This stems in part from social capital's implicit and sometimes explicit emphasis on consensus versus ("healthy") competition in politics, on the civic rather than the political, and its underplaying the situation of racial minorities by emphasizing the circumstances of whites. The importance of continuing scholarly and practical attention to the impact of race as a factor that profoundly conditions America's notions of community is clear, especially with increasing ethnic complexity (immigration is certainly an important development, but one that is not specifically addressed in the present inquiry; cf. King 2000).

As scholars and the public seek to appreciate the past development and continuing evolution of the American political system and its aspirations for democracy and equality, it seems that coming to grips with (and better understanding) the full importance of racial/ethnic diversity is more urgent than dwelling on what we show to be the romantic versions of civic republicanism – particularly when systematic evidence casts so much doubt on the social capital thesis (Hero 2003a). Although continuing to consider the juxtaposition and interaction of racial diversity and social capital (and other factors) is a worthy enterprise, more attention should be addressed to the former than the latter because, as we shall see, the theory and evidence provided in this book make clear the larger impact of racial diversity in American politics from the mid-twentieth century to the present – and probably before that as well. Ever-increasing and perhaps more complex diversity make such research especially necessary.

I begin the discussion, then, in the spirit of inquiry and pursuit of understanding what I believe are fundamental questions of empirical democratic theory, given important normative underpinnings, and their implications for American politics.

2

The Social Capital Thesis

The quality and durability of democracy in the United States have often been attributed in significant part to its "civil society," sense of "community," and, in more contemporary terminology, "social capital." Discussed long ago by Tocqueville (1835) and echoed by other prominent scholars over the years, assertions that rich and dense networks of social interaction are and have been linchpins of U.S. democracy are strongly restated and affirmed in a number of major recent works (Putnam 2000, 1995, Skocpol et al. 2000; cf. Elazar 1966, 1972, 1984; Rice and Sumberg 1997; Knack 2002). Indeed, the social capital thesis has become a major influence and a prominent school of thought in the study of American and comparative politics, advanced by a number of scholars (Putnam 1995, 2000; Skocpol 2003; Crowley and Skocpol 2001; cf. Rice and Sumberg 1997). (Social capital theory has also been a major focus of research in other disciplines, such as sociology and economics; here, however, I will examine its impact only in political science scholarship.) Social capital and related concepts, such as "political culture" and "civic culture," are said – and ostensibly demonstrated to be – essential correlates of procedural and substantive democracy and of civic and economic equality in America, historically and into the present.

The social capital thesis as developed by Robert Putnam (2000) concerning the role of civil society, particularly claims about social capital's significance for the society's general well-being, has received extraordinary scholarly and popular attention. That thesis initially emerged in a widely heralded and highly influential study of Italy, *Making Democracy Work: Civic Traditions in Modern Italy* (Putnam 1993). The argument was later further developed and applied to the United States, first in brief, article form and then in a full-length book, *Bowling Alone: The Collapse and Revival of American Community* (Putnam 2000; hereafter referred to as "*BA*"). The first book (1993) delineated the correlates of democracy in Italy, particularly the importance of civil society as operationally defined in the concept of "social capital" (cf. Tarrow 1996). The second book represents the most elaborate statement of social capital's purportedly profound and beneficial impacts in American society and provides massive empirical evidence and systematic evaluation. The analysis in *BA* has, it seems fair to say, set the standard and become the authoritative source of social capital studies and social outcomes in political science research on the United States. For these reasons, the arguments contained in *BA* are discussed extensively in this chapter and throughout the book, and *BA* is accordingly used as the major reference on social capital.

The social capital argument is deeply concerned with "community" and "civic virtue" (Putnam 2000, p. 19), their ostensible decline in America, and, in turn, with the erosion of civic association, the declining social trust and social isolation, and the economic inequality that are said to have accompanied this decline. The reason the decline is so disturbing is that social capital is said to have many and profound salutary effects, as evidence provided in the study seems to demonstrate. *Bowling Alone* also stresses and confronts the historic tension in American political ideas between community and individualism, suggesting that the particular form(s) of individualism that emerged in the mid-1960s are especially troublesome. Moreover, the importance of the role of race in shaping American civic culture, society, and politics is frequently and firmly acknowledged. But as I shall emphasize, the way that race is (or is not) considered in the actual empirical analysis – in other words, how it is (or is not) represented in the central questions (dependent variables) and as potential explanatory factors (independent variables) – means that its role is almost certainly understated in major social capital studies.

Bowling Alone provides a thorough and thoughtful assessment of social capital's vital role in American politics, and the book's broader relevance for democratic theory is readily apparent. But *BA* is not the first or only such argument of its kind; there are others of a similar bent, some of which will be discussed in this chapter as well (cf., e.g., Elazar 1972, 1984; also see Stolle and Hooghe 2005). *Bowling Alone*'s essential argument is that because of the nation's rich social capital – most notably manifest in the attitudes, behavior, and civic volunteerism of the generation born before 1930 – American democracy functioned quite effectively during most of its history; this is alleged to have certainly been the case during much of twentieth century until the mid-1960s and was perhaps most evident in the World War II generation. That is, extensive and nurturing social connections through civic association are said to have facilitated norms of reciprocity and social trust that deeply enriched American society, leading to a host of salutary effects (Putnam 2000, p. 19).

Social capital contributes to democracy in two different ways, according to Putnam (2000, p. 338). "Externally, voluntary associations ... allow individuals to express their interests and demands on government and to protect themselves from abuses of power from political leaders. Political information flows through social networks, and in these networks public life is discussed" (cf. Knack 2002). At the same time, "Internally, associations and less formal networks of civic engagement instill in their members habits of cooperation and public-spiritedness, as well as the practical skills necessary to partake in public life" (cf. Verba, Schlozman, and Brady 1995).

The core empirical analyses in *BA* address two basic issues. One concerns *why* social capital declined in the first place. The other issue concerns the *consequences* of high social capital, which are found to be resoundingly beneficial, along with the implications of its erosion. *Bowling Alone* first extensively documents the "collapse" of social capital, which begins to be evident in the late sixties and early seventies, and then turns to examining and explaining the decline. In a nutshell, *BA* argues that the weakening of social capital was attributable to and primarily exacerbated by "generational change." Generational change was abetted by and intertwined with the impact of television, along with urban sprawl and work (Putnam 2000, ch. 15), as social forces that led to widespread civic *dis*engagement and social isolation. According to Putnam, the World War II generation was especially civic-minded, and its diminishing presence and ongoing replacement by subsequent generations seriously undermined the overall civic orientation in American society. The generations that were born or reached adulthood in the mid- to late 1950s and thereafter have lacked the civic commitment of their predecessors for various reasons, including social change wrought by the isolating effects of electronic media, suburbanization, and changing family lifestyles (Putnam 2000).

As important as discerning the causes of civic decline may be in *BA*, a great deal of space is devoted to the "so what" question, that is, the consequences of social capital. The consequences of social capital are the overriding concern in the current study (although the "why" question will be touched upon as well). When considering the implications of social capital for social and political outcomes, *BA* focuses on the states of the United States, drawing mostly on data from the 1980s and 1990s (see especially Chapters 16–20 and also Chapters 21–22); the current study will do likewise.

In order to systematically assess this social capital thesis, Putnam developed a "social capital index" (for 1990), which serves as the major explanatory (independent) variable regarding the contemporary importance of civic republicanism and community for various aspects of American society and politics (Putnam 2000, chs. 16–22). This social capital index has five components and fourteen specific variables; the components include measures of community organizational life, engagement in public affairs, community volunteerism, informal sociability, and social trust (Putnam 2000, p. 291). These components and variables are combined into the social capital index and serve as markers of social behaviors and attitudes, which are then examined relative to an array of social and political outcomes. The central claim: where there is (and has been) more aggregate social capital, there is greater sense of community and, perhaps most significantly, markedly better social outcomes (cf. Fishman 2004). Social capital is a "lubricant," fostering cooperation that leads to these desirable results. Accordingly, when the United States has had higher levels of social capital (i.e., before the mid-1960s), various social, economic, and political conditions were clearly "better." Although sense of community and better social outcomes are the emphasis in *BA*, an important spillover effect – a strong link between social capital and *equality*, especially certain dimensions of equality – is also asserted. In short, the study makes a series of forceful assertions about social capital's impact on substantive policies, procedural democracy, and social equality. We now turn to an examination of these claims.

IMPACTS OF SOCIAL CAPITAL

Bowling Alone focuses on evidence from the American states in considering the consequences of social capital levels for social and political outcomes; as mentioned previously, data for the variables to be explained (dependent variables) are generally from the 1990s. The numerous analyses of social capital's impact on social outcomes send a clear and powerful message: higher social capital is strongly related to a vast array of beneficial outcomes. Social capital is often shown to provide the leading explanation of outcomes, even after accounting for such factors as states' overall racial composition and poverty levels. Thus, for various indicators of child welfare and educational performance (Putnam 2000, ch. 17), safe and productive neighborhoods (ch. 18), economic prosperity (ch. 19), and health and happiness (ch. 20), higher levels of social capital are strongly related to better outcomes. To wit: "kids are better off in high social capital states," "schools work better in high social capital states," "health is better in high social capital states"; furthermore, "social capital and tolerance go together" (p. 356). *Bowling Alone* understandably heralds these findings, often noting the "astonishingly" strong relationships between levels of social capital and the outcomes studied (see chs. 16–20). Factors such as poverty, racial composition, and education do also appear to have some modest impacts on the outcomes, but these are not discussed extensively, given the focus on social capital.

The findings that social capital so profoundly affects so many outcomes and elements are highly impressive and warrant the most serious consideration. Indeed, *BA*'s findings are even more impressive because of their consistency with other findings on *aggregate* patterns of social outcomes in certain social settings (cf. Hero 1998; Elazar 1972, 1984).

Along with assertions that higher social capital is strongly associated with better substantive outcomes (Putnam 2000, chs. 16–20), a strong link between social capital and equality, especially civic and economic dimensions of equality, is posited (pp. 358–63 and ch. 22). Specifically: "the American states with the highest levels of social capital are precisely the states most characterized by economic and civic equality." An examination in the states of relationships between social capital and measures of economic and civic equality – measured with gini coefficients and a civic equality index, respectively – finds that social capital strongly "goes together" with civic and economic equality (pp. 360–1). With specific reference to economic and civic equality, Putnam declares: "Both across space, and across time, equality and fraternity [community] are strongly positively correlated" (p. 359). Indeed, it is emphatically argued that equality and community are connected: "the empirical evidence on recent trends is *unambiguous*.... *Community and equality are mutually reinforcing, not mutually incompatible*" (p. 358, emphasis in original; also see Elazar 1984; Rice and Sumberg 1997). In short, the assertion can be interpreted as suggesting that one core element of the American political tradition, civic republicanism as embodied in "social capital," plays a pivotal role in relation to an element of another tradition, the egalitarian tradition (see Smith 1993), in mitigating economic ("class") inequality.

A cautionary note is added, however. Despite the massive evidence marshalled and the strong and consistent findings, the argument is said to be "neither exhaustive nor conclusive," and scholarship in various fields is exploring the "correlates and consequences of social capital. Much more work will be needed to prove the power of social capital and, in particular, to show in detail how and when its effects are clearest and most beneficial" (Putnam 2000, pp. 294–5). There have indeed been a number of studies focusing on various dimensions of politics and policy that have taken up this call for additional research.

Other studies, both subsequent and prior to the publication of *BA*, bear strong similarities to the social capital thesis and have drawn comparable conclusions about social and political outcomes. Of equal importance is that these other studies share certain problematic conceptual and analytical traits with the social capital argument, as I shall discuss later. For now I merely summarize some of these to illustrate the themes, spirit, and findings of this body of research, which includes empirical applications growing out of civic republican orientations. The purpose here is suggest the breadth of substantive questions examined from social capital or civic culture perspectives, the similarities and differences in conceptualizing social capital and measuring it as an independent variable, and the range of findings and conclusions that emerge. For the most part such research takes the social capital thesis "on its own terms," primarily seeking to test the core arguments as articulated in major works. That is, these studies typically do not set out to challenge the basic assumptions or premises of social capital but instead seek to refine, clarify, and perhaps extend the thesis. They commonly produce evidence that supports the social capital thesis and/or similar arguments, although some of the findings do depart from social capital's claims to some degree.

OTHER SOCIAL CAPITAL EMPIRICAL STUDIES

Social capital has been applied to – and found to have important effects on – aspects of politics well beyond the numerous dimensions identified in *BA*. One study examined the impact of social capital on the "quality" and "performance" of state governments (Knack 2002). Its measures of states' social capital included: volunteering, percentage of citizens who respond to census questionnaires, social trust, informal socializing, club meetings, and membership in "good government" groups. Quality and performance essentially equates to government accountability and efficiency, whose measurement was based on the adoption and implementation of a number of administrative practices such as financial management, capital management, human resources, managing for results, and information technology. These factors make for an interesting comparison with Putnam's measurement of social capital (cf. Fishman 2004).

The quality of state administrative practice, according to Knack, both reflects and furthers the openness and trust in government that one would expect to be associated with social capital. The central finding is that indicators of states' level of social capital are in fact generally related to some of the indicators of government quality that are examined separately. He also finds that the percentage of African Americans in a state's population is positively associated with government performance and that income inequality has a consistently negative significant effect; indeed, these two variables are as consistently related to the dependent variables as is social capital. That race and economic inequality have such consistent impact – and perhaps even more so since they have the *opposite* effect – is certainly intriguing. However, given the emphasis on social capital, the findings on the impact of race and of economic inequality are not discussed much.

In general, then, Knack's (2002) study clearly supports the social capital thesis, albeit with qualifications. It finds that aspects of social capital identified with "generalized reciprocity" (such as social trust, volunteering, and willingness to respond to census takers) are in fact associated with better governmental performance. On the other hand, aspects of social capital identified with "social connectedness" (including activity in associations and informal socializing) are generally *not* related to governmental performance, with membership in "good government" groups the notable exception. The broad affirmation of the social capital thesis – and distinguishing the importance of "generalized" trust versus the "connectedness" dimensions of the concept – are noteworthy.

These conclusions, as qualified, lend support to the cautions of social capital researchers that not all groups and associations are necessarily equally beneficial to general well-being. Putnam distinguishes "bonding" (i.e., exclusive and inwardly focused) groups from "bridging" groups – that is, inclusive, open groups that reach out to others and that are ostensibly focused on a larger public good. Theiss-Morse and Hibbing (2005) make a parallel claim more forcefully in challenging the social capital thesis, contending that individuals are strongly inclined to join associations and groups of like-minded and socially similar individuals (also see Chapter 7 herein) and are more strongly disposed to bonding, consensual associations than to bridging, competitive relations.

A study designed to directly test the bonding–bridging distinction assessed the impact of bridging and bonding association on the responsiveness of elected officials to the mass public in 64 American communities (Hill and Matsubayashi 2005), using data from the early 1970s (which is about when social capital began to decline, according to Putnam). Hence this study, like Knack's, examines connections between social capital and governmental behavior. As such, Hill and Matsubayashi may go beyond issues considered by most social capital analysis, which does not address actions of formal governmental institutions per se (as we argue in Chapter 6), but their analysis seems consistent with the spirit of *BA*'s arguments.

Guided by suggestions offered in *BA*, Hill and Matsubayashi categorized "fraternal organizations, labor unions, fraternities, sororities, farm organizations, study clubs, and professional societies as bonding groups" and "service clubs, veterans organizations, political organizations, sports associations, school service organizations, and hobby organizations as bridging groups" (2005, p. 218). They found that "membership in bridging social capital associations is *unrelated*" to public officials' responsiveness; this is not consistent with social capital's claims. They also found that "bonding social capital membership is *negatively associated* with" governmental responsiveness (emphases added); this is in some ways consistent with Putnam's specific caveats about a potential "dark side" of social capital but does not necessarily affirm his more general arguments. In short, this study offered little support for the claims about beneficial effects of social capital but strong evidence indicating negative effects of bonding group membership on representation.

In some contrast to Hill and Matsubayashi (2005), Brehm and Rahn's (1997) study of individual-level effects of social capital finds that "civic engagement and interpersonal trust are in a tight reciprocal relationship, where the connection is stronger from participation to interpersonal trust rather than the reverse," and more trust and engagement are associated with greater confidence in government. The direct implications of this study for general social connectedness and/or broad social outcomes and matters of equality is less obvious.

Other studies, spurred in part by the spirit of Putnam's early formulations of the social capital thesis (1993), undertook an analysis of "civic culture" – a notion essentially similar to the concept of social capital – and its impact on government performance in the American states (Rice and Sumberg 1997). This inquiry found "a clear link between civicness and performance." These measures of civic culture, which are similar to Putnam's and Knack's formulations of social capital, include four components and eleven specific indicators (Rice and Sumberg 1997, p. 105). One component, *engagement*, is measured by newspaper circulation per capita, library books per capita in public libraries, community improvement and philanthropy/voluntarism groups per capita, and the gender distribution of public school teachers. Another component, *equality*, includes percentage of state legislators who are women, civil rights groups per capita of nonwhites, and income inequality. A third, called *solidarity, trust, and tolerance*, includes crime rate, lawyers per capita, and default rate on Perkins student loans. A final component of this civic culture indicator, *social structures of cooperation*, is "a per capita composite index of twenty-six different types of nonprofit organizations." The authors assess the impact of civic culture on government performance.

Rice and Sumberg (1997) employ three indicators of government performance, which differ somewhat from those used by others. *Policy liberalism* refers to "the extent to which societies have adopted the types of policies generally associated with modern liberalism, such as extensive welfare systems, progressive tax structures, and consumer protections standards." They use "a ranking of states that combines eight policy measures" that "reflect the usual ideological divisions between liberals and conservatives." A second aspect of government performance is *innovation*, which they analyze with data "from a comprehensive index of state policy creativity based on more than sixty types of policies." The third indicator, *administrative effectiveness*, is based on an average of two indices, one of the "quality of state administration" and one of "the capacity of state government legislatures to make effective and efficient decisions."

Examining the central questions within this framework, Rice and Sumberg conclude that a "link between [civic] culture and [government] performance is indisputable" and, moreover, that "the strength of the relationship between civic culture and government performance in the states is pronounced" (1997, pp. 109–10). These findings hold even when a number of other variables are considered, including a measure of state "diversity," which is found to have no impact itself. It is perhaps telling that the diversity measure used in this civic culture (social capital) study was from 1973 and was based on "percent foreign born" in a state; this is a questionable measure given that minority groups – the vast majority of African Americans, most Latinos who trace their ancestry to the American Southwest, and Native Americans – would not be counted in this measure of diversity. In any case, these findings affirming social capital claims are another in a tradition of similar analyses associated with political and civic culture in America (but see Hero 2003b).

Elazar's "political culture" thesis (1972, 1984) chronologically preceded and in many ways conceptually anticipated the social capital argument; indeed, several times Putnam notes the strong similarities and strong statistical correlations between social capital and political culture. Political culture was also a precursor to the Rice and Sumberg (1997) study of civic culture, as those authors note. The thesis deserves attention here because of its broad and continuing theoretical influence. Elazar delineated three U.S. political cultures, which are rooted in historical settlement and migration patterns of European settlers across the country and created belief systems and legacies that continue to deeply influence American politics. Elazar discusses and explains his view of the sources of state political cultures – religious and ethnic (especially European) groups – and provides concepts and categories. But he goes well beyond that, and some researchers question the adequacy or accuracy of Elazar's historical assumptions and arguments.

Elazar claims that in one culture "the political order is conceived to be a commonwealth – a state in which the people have an undivided interest – in which the citizens cooperate to create and maintain the best government in order to implement certain shared moral principles" (Elazar 1984, p. 112); he calls this the *moralistic* culture. In another, the political order is conceived as a marketplace in which "the primary public relationships are products of bargaining among individuals and groups out of self-interest"; this is labeled the *individualistic* culture. These two conceptions broadly parallel the civic republican and the liberal tradition, respectively, as described by Smith (1993). The third, *traditionalistic,* culture is said to be rooted in an "ambivalent attitude toward the marketplace coupled with a paternalistic and elitist conception of the commonwealth." Elazar's fuller description, and his argument that the traditionalistic culture is most evident in the southern and southwestern states, suggest that the traditionalistic subculture is the clearest example of – and certainly parallels – the third tradition identified by Smith (1993, 1997): ascriptive hierarchy or inegalitarianism. But in an interesting contrast to Smith (1993, 1997), Elazar identified only two philosophical *traditions*; the third, which Elazar neither discusses directly nor applies to racial inequality, is the ascriptive inegalitarianism of racial hierarchy ideas.

Though specifying only two theoretical traditions, Elazar claims there are three subcultures evident in the American states, each reflecting "its own particular synthesis of the marketplace and the commonwealth." Elazar's description of the commonwealth orientation of the "moralistic" subculture clearly evokes a civic republican, civic virtue, or communitarian orientation, very much like Putnam's claims about rich and dense social capital – although Putnam points to differences only in the levels of aggregate social capital and does not delineate separate political cultures substantively. The marketplace–exchange and interest-based features of an "individualistic" orientation shares important similarities with liberalism (as described by Smith 1993) and is suggestive of the type of thinking that, to the distress of social capital theorists, came to dominate American civil society after the 1960s and so undermined social capital. Elazar's account of the roots and orientation of the "traditionalistic" subculture is, however, less clear and arguably not well developed. In a sense, Elazar noted one (almost entirely) positive and two somewhat less desirable political cultures: moralistic on the one hand and, on the other, individualistic and traditionalistic.

Elazar (much as Putnam would later) argues and provides evidence, although somewhat impressionistic and anecdotal in nature, that political culture has broad and deep implications for a large number and various dimensions of state politics and policies. These include: general views of orientations toward politics (again, commonwealth, individualism, traditionalism); what are seen as the appropriate spheres of governmental activity (broader, though with nongovernmental approaches preferred, versus narrower); greater or lesser receptiveness to new programs and policy innovation; how bureaucracy is viewed (negatively, ambivalently, or positively because fairness is encouraged in rule-based decision making; cf. Knack 2002); the kind of civil service system (merit-based vs. patronage); how politics is viewed (as healthy, as dirty, or as a privilege for a relative few); who should participate (everyone? professionals? the appropriate elite?); the role of political parties; party cohesiveness; and the kinds and nature of party competition (oriented toward issues, material interest, or the status quo). Elazar asserts that moralistic (commonwealth) settings produce better outcomes; less positive outcomes occur in individualistic or traditionalistic contexts, though to different degrees and in different ways (here outcomes seem to be "bad" or "ugly").

The breadth and nature of the alleged impact of political culture, perhaps most notably where the commonwealth ideas prevail, are impressive and are strikingly similar to assertions that social capital (or civic culture) has profound impacts on a wide range of social and political processes and outcomes (Elazar 1984; see Putnam 2000, p. 495; Rice and Sumberg 1997; Knack 2002).

Elazar's thesis engendered a tremendous body of research and has had much appeal to many scholars of state politics because, according to some (see Gray 1999, 1996), it is "consistent with popular impressions about state differences in political values, style and tone"; that idea also influenced social capital perspectives. The same can be said about the social capital thesis, which in turn has gained much more visibility and popularity with intellectual and popular audiences. Another reason for the influence of Elazar's cultural argument and the social capital thesis is, we suggest, their comprehensiveness in identifying ostensible effects on a broad array of state social, political, and governmental phenomena.

Other work, some of which is sympathetic to the political culture interpretation, has questioned Elazar's specific terminology and has also leveled major criticisms at Elazar's basic understanding of culture and history in the United States. Thompson et al. (1990) argue that Elazar's term "moralistic" is misleading in several ways and suggest that this culture really seems to entail "egalitarian communalism." They also suggest that the "traditionalistic" category be reconceived as "hierarchical collectivism," a context where there is "a place for everyone, and everyone in their place." These are important refinements and suggest at least two points.

First, they indicate that Elazar's moralistic and traditionalistic cultures *both* have forms of collective or communal orientations. Also suggested is that a supposed central feature of the moralistic culture is an emphasis on "equality" – including, according to some, not just equality of opportunity but even equality of outcomes (cf. Hanson 1994). However, such equality may be most evident in particular settings that vary as a function of competing interpretations. At the same time, the hierarchical collectivism or notion of community suggested in traditionalistic cultures seems akin to what Putnam refers to as a prevalence of bonding associations that may also involve the so-called dark side of social capital. It is interesting that most political culture analyses give little attention to racial inequality (see Thompson et al. 1990). Elazar scarcely acknowledged race at all; and actual social capital analyses do not stress race, notwithstanding various comments offered concerning its importance (Putnam 2000).

The captivating and broad-ranging nature of the political culture framework generated a great deal of research, as did the social capital thesis later. Writing some time ago, Lieske (1993) asserted that over a hundred studies had directly used the political culture argument. And Nardulli (1990), in a study that ultimately found virtually no support for the political culture thesis, offered that "no self-respecting regression analysis concerned with state politics can ignore" the Elazar scale. The array of issues that have been examined relative to political culture is likewise impressive; and social capital work has generated a great amount of scholarly and popular interest. Also striking is how frequently research finds that political culture is a significant factor in understanding state politics and policies.

Though research often finds support for the Elazar framework, some scholars claim that such support is mixed. Thompson et al. (1990) believe that how well Elazar's theory has withstood scrutiny "is a matter of continuing debate." For every study that claims to have found Elazar's theory vindicated, there is another that claims to find it of little use. Gray (1999, 1996), who generally lauds the political culture thesis (and also asserts its prominence and plausibility over social diversity arguments, ignoring much evidence to the contrary), notes an apparent disjunction between aggregate- and individual-level findings regarding political culture. Existing work on political culture and state politics has not been able to reconcile differences between individual-level and aggregate-level findings on a number of issues. Stone et al. (2001) offer an explanation of why social capital may be similarly ambiguous; this, in turn, echoes Knack's (2002) distinction between "generalized reciprocity" and "social connectedness dimensions" of social capital and his claim that the former but not the latter affect government performance. Despite its apparent focus on social dimensions, "Social capital concerns behavior that is largely interpersonal and private" and not necessarily "activities that are squarely in the public arena and involve governance institutions and major group representatives." With regard to a large public arena, "habits of cooperation [in contrast to such inclinations as the skills, social trust, and reciprocity associated with social capital] that develop in small and close meetings do not necessarily come into play" (Stone et al. 2001, pp. 5–6).

SOCIAL CAPITAL, POLITICAL/CIVIC CULTURE, AND RACE

The seriousness, vigor, and breadth of the theoretical and empirical work in Putnam's eloquent and massive study (*BA*) are impressive; one can offer similar plaudits to other works in the political culture and social capital tradition of the study of American politics (e.g., Elazar 1984; Rice and Sumberg 1997). Assertions about the connection of social capital to salutary outcomes and equality seem initially powerful and persuasive at a general level and with respect to numerous dimensions of social outcomes and equality. The contrast between the strong and allegedly corrosive individualistic tendencies of the post-1960s American culture and the civic republican or community orientation that supposedly prevailed in earlier eras – and most powerfully in the World War II generation – is certainly arresting. But Putnam is also sensitive to another strand of American ideas, one that fostered inequalities of race and social class (what Smith would refer to as the racial hierarchy or inegalitarian tradition).

Bowling Alone clearly and forcefully acknowledges the importance of race in American politics a number of times.

Bowling Alone asserts: "Race is such a fundamental feature
of American social history that nearly every other feature of our
society is connected to it in some way" (Putnam 2000, p. 279);
also, "Race is the most important embodiment of the ethical
crosscurrents that swirl around the rocks of social capital in contemporary America" (p. 361). I suspect that few would disagree
with these points. On the other hand, in its actual analysis *BA*
does not appropriately incorporate race/ethnicity considerations
and measures into its larger framework and specific assessments.
More problematically, a large body of research that *has* explicitly
and extensively done so is ignored.

The statements of concern about race in *BA* are not pursued
with methodological approaches or specific analyses that properly account for racial and ethnic factors. Most significantly, the
empirical assessments never directly incorporate race into the
central dependent variables – that is, the indicators of the numerous social outcomes (e.g., degree of civic equality) at the heart
of the argument. Moreover, the core independent variable of
social capital also obscures the potential impact of racial factors
(Putnam 2000; cf. Hero 2003a). Other social capital analyses
scarcely acknowledge the relevance of race in American politics
(cf. Rice and Sumberg 1997; Elazar 1972, 1984; also see the discussion in Hero 2003a). Because race has been such an integral
part of American civil society, to recognize its importance but
then neglect it in actual empirical analysis strongly suggests that
social capital arguments should be reconsidered (King and Smith
2005).

The social outcome indicators do not differentiate outcomes
for racial minorities versus others; the consequences of this for
understanding racial inequality are considerable when the size
of minority populations differs so much across the states. And
neither the "civic equality index" nor the measure of economic
inequality (gini coefficients) are disaggregated with respect to

race (Putnam 2000; cf. Rice and Sumberg 1997). As a result, racial and ethnic aspects are rendered largely invisible, and their potential impact on American civil society is "designed out" of the analysis. Analyses offered in support of social capital's claims regarding equality do not consider certain elements of substantive and civic economic equality; conspicuously absent are potential racial dimensions. Neither do the analyses distinguish "bonding" (exclusive) from "bridging" (inclusive) social capital, an admittedly difficult task, and the evidence marshalled does not speak to racial "bridging" or differences. Yet to fully understand American civil society, we must consider social capital's underlying composition, configurations, and distributions – including how these are related to race – and not only the aggregate levels, as is typically the case with social capital analyses (Orr 1999; Hero 1998, 2003b; cf. Putnam 2000; Rice and Sumberg 1997).

Assertions about the civic nature of American society during much of the 1900s (and earlier), despite the ample evidence of formal and informal inequality that challenges those assertions, is "vivid testimony" to its overlooking the prominence of certain forms of racial inequality (notwithstanding the numerous allusions to race noted previously; cf. Smith 1993, pp. 551–3). But this is not surprising in light of Smith's assertion that "omission or minimization of excluded groups characterize every author in the Tocquevillian [civic republican/community] tradition" (1993, p. 557). That is, philosophical works in that tradition commonly understate the implications of racial/ethnic factors in American politics. And social capital's orientation certainly seeks to provide evidence that would affirm the "civic republican" tradition.

In a more pronounced fashion, a predecessor to social capital – Elazar's political culture – scarcely discussed the presence or the beliefs of minority groups (see Hero 1998), although later extensions of Elazar's work do address this. Indeed, Lieske's analysis of "regional subcultures" (1993) does so specifically, though the dependent variables he examined do not consider racial/ethnic outcomes (cf. Hero 1998, pp. 33–5). Similarly, Rice and Sumberg (1997), who link political culture and social capital perspectives, largely ignore race as factor, and the indicator of "diversity" they use is questionable (as already noted). In the case of *BA*, the racial bases and potential biases of social capital seem not to be adequately considered (as I shall demonstrate), and this deficiency is further exacerbated and perhaps caused by inattention to relevant previous research on race and ethnicity.

The overall characterization in *BA* of the period from 1900 to the early 1960s is no less than benign and is often effusively positive (see also Chapter 7 herein). But there are obvious reasons to pause about this. Formal racial segregation and other types of discrimination existed both de jure and de facto for most of the period described as being highly civic. For instance, Burns (1994) affirms that restrictive covenants affecting residential housing and developments, which were typically formulated and enforced by groups known simply as "neighborhood improvement associations," were a major mechanism for racial residential segregation until the Supreme Court struck down such practices in 1948 (Jones-Correa 2000). These neighborhood improvement associations might fit well among the community organizations touted by various works in the social capital tradition. Following the Court's 1948 decision – that is, beginning in the early 1950s, a period seen in *BA* as part of the highly civic era – the very creation and form of local municipalities and special district governments were often mechanisms of racial and economic separation (Hayward 2003), led again by arguably (self-styled) civic-oriented groups.

Bowling Alone argues that the general collapse of social capital in the United States occurred in the 1960s. However, when assessing levels of social capital across the states, it argues that there has been considerable stability in the patterns (although the aggregate levels have declined). Implied, but not clearly stated or demonstrated, is that the declining levels of social capital occurred similarly across the states. This begs the question of what created the broader original patterns. *Bowling Alone* directly invokes Elazar's "political culture" thesis, although Putnam brings more direct attention to the history of slavery and to ethnic diversity than did Elazar (see Lieske 1993; Hero 1998). *Bowling Alone* notes that the "clear historical continuities" in the patterns of social capital lead to the question of whether social capital is a cause or merely an effect of contemporary social circumstance:

> If regional and local patterns of civic engagement and social connectedness were evanescent and mutable, then correlations between social capital and other social facts ... might well reflect the *effect* of those factors on social capital. If, on the other hand, regional and local profiles of social capital represent long-standing traditions, then it is more plausible that social capital is a *cause*, not merely an *effect*, of contemporary social circumstance." (Putnam 2000, p. 294, emphasis in original)

Although race has been a constant in American history, its specific manifestations and implications have differed over time and have varied across states and localities. In *BA* this is recognized at a general level but is never fully reconciled with the broader argument, either theoretically or empirically. This is understandable in part because such matters are not easily addressed. However, social capital approaches often ignore previous theorizing and a large body of evidence that have sought to grapple with these very issues.

As noted earlier, *BA* does discuss the

> risk that *emphasizing community exacerbates division and exclusion*. Since social capital is *inevitably easier to foster within homogeneous communities*, emphasis on its creation may inadvertently shift the balance away from bridging social capital and toward bonding social capital. (Putnam 2000, p. 400, emphases added)

It is interesting to observe that certain work that seems to contradict this point is noted approvingly: citing others, Putnam (2000) offers that "Other things being equal, the more economically, ethnically, and religiously heterogeneous the membership of an association is, the greater its capacity to cultivate the kind of public discourse and deliberation that is conducive to democratic citizenship." In any case, *BA* acknowledges – but may not fully incorporate and seems ultimately to underappreciate – that civil society and social capital are as much about relations *between* groups, between racial communities. Not including racial/ethnic group relations and not sufficiently emphasizing that such relations commonly do not take place on equal footing is a problem (Knack 2002). Orr (1999), for example, has shown that blacks developed high social capital (in Baltimore) in large part to form a "solidary" defense against legal and informal discrimination from whites; however, white social capital and its associated political power and authority prevented black social capital from being fully conveyed to broader civic and political arenas. Other research indicates that relatively high social capital does not necessarily work the same for other groups, either; networks may lead "nowhere" (Schneider et al. 1997). Civic engagement and disengagement may take various forms, and they might be expected to vary by context and for different groups within a given context. As developed in later chapters, the story may be different when one recognizes that social capital is highest where the populations are most homogeneous (least racially diverse) and when one examines the effects of social capital on various groups relative to each other.

For the most part, Putnam dismisses the role of ethnic factors and the renegotiation of minority status in his discussion of the decline of social capital in the 1960s because (1) racial differences in associational membership are not large and (2) the erosion of social capital has affected all races. It is also argued that (3) civic disengagement viewed as white flight from community life after the civil rights revolution is hard to reconcile with the generational differences:

Why should disengagement be hardly visible at all among Americans who came of age in the first half of the century, when American society was objectively more segregated and subjectively more racist than in the 1960s and 1970s?

If racial prejudice were responsible for America's civic disengagement, disengagement ought to be most pronounced among the most bigoted individuals and generations. But it is not. (2000, p. 280)

Some thoughts come to mind in response to this assertion. Although differences in associational membership across racial groups may not be large, one should not just assume that all associations (and hence associational memberships) were created equal to begin with. Depending on the number and strength of associational activities, declines may be less or more debilitating to groups and their individual members. Furthermore, although the erosion of social capital is alleged to have affected all races, that may matter more for some groups than for others depending on their starting point, where they "stood" to begin with. The lower their starting point – in terms not only of social capital but also of education, socioeconomic status, and the like – the more damaging erosion would presumably be. And perhaps there was less disengagement by members of earlier, "civic" generations because the social networks to which they belonged were stronger and already well established and hence were less directly affected by the social and generational changes that may have led to social capital's decline. The data provided in *BA* are not specific enough to offer assurances that the civic generation's continued engagement was entirely (or even primarily) in bridging organizations or that it may have been in bonding associations.

Moreover, the decline of social capital could be explained not only by generational replacement but also by *who* is part of the later generations. That is, the post-1960s generation was more open to groups – that is, blacks and other racial minorities – that previously had been constrained or had been excluded from the American social system and formal arenas of the political system. Members of these formally excluded groups, whose social capital presumably had been weakened by long-term exclusion and social inequality, might well be less engaged (at least in the early periods of their formal inclusion) in terms of the way that social capital and civic culture arguments conceive and measure their core concepts.

SOCIAL CAPITAL AND ITS DECLINE

Bowling Alone's dismissal of the impact of racial factors in the collapse of social capital is hard to refute directly, but on its face it seems difficult to reconcile with findings on the contemporary correlates of social capital and social diversity (presented later). For the moment, I simply reiterate how remarkable it is that social capital's decline occurred about the same time as – but is said not to be at all connected to – the adoption of the Civil Rights Act of 1964, the Voting Rights Act of 1965 (which was renewed and expanded in 1975 to include "linguistic minorities"), the Equal Pay Act (1963), the full incorporation of the Bill of Rights into state laws, the 1965 immigration legislation, the "reapportionment revolution" of the 1960s, the beginnings of Affirmative Action, urban riots, challenges to reformed urban governmental structures (often including at-large elections), and state legislatures' typically incremental moves from amateur to professional bodies, to name some of the most obvious. Indeed, one could argue that the very purpose of the major legislation and other changes was in fact to undercut existing social practices and institutions that had been established and authorized through prevailing social networks and norms – in other words, social capital – and that were biased and unequal with regard to race, class, and gender and so contradicted basic liberal values (see Klinkner and Smith 1999). (The policy changes were not necessarily justified in the specific language of eroding social capital, however.) Some research has suggested that the decline of PTA/PTO activities was higher in states that experienced desegregation (Crawford and Levitt 1999), but further evidence of this sort has not emerged. Perhaps the lessening of a group's exclusivity, which is part of what made the group appealing to some of its members, played a role in declining memberships (see Theiss-Morse and Hibbing 2005).

It is also notable that while social capital may have decreased, democracy – or at least procedural democracy – has certainly increased, in large part because of the numerous policies and social change just noted. For example, Hill's (1994) analysis of "democracy in the fifty states" indicates significantly increased democracy over time. There is much more democracy – defined as guarantees of the right to vote, degree of party competition, and levels of voter turnout – in the 1980s than the 1940s, though the former period (according to *BA*) was much more civic and had higher social capital than the latter.

Similarly, Erikson et al. (1993) suggest that democracy, defined as public policies that reflect the ideological orientations and preferences of citizens, is generally enhanced by greater political party competition, which was more widespread after the sixties than before. The processes may work differently in different political settings, but to the extent those contexts or cultures are themselves significantly shaped by racial diversity, the social capital thesis is less persuasive. However, observe that Hill (1994) and Erikson et al. (1993) view rights, such as the right to vote, and competition, particularly political party competition, as essential elements of democracy; in contrast, social capital visions of democracy are more rooted in community and consensus. In short, there are different versions of (or at least different emphases on) what democracy requires and entails in social capital versus other perspectives. These findings suggest a greater disjunction between equality and social capital than is often recognized.

There may be other plain evidence for reservations about the social capital thesis. Most who are familiar with the American states would quickly recognize that those with high social capital (see Putnam 2000, p. 293) tend to be sparsely populated or racially/ethnically homogeneous or, most commonly, both. In particular, North Dakota, South Dakota, Vermont, Montana, and Minnesota constitute the top five (the top 10 percent) of states in terms of levels of social capital; yet these states are clearly not representative of America's racial composition and economic complexity, and they are among the least populated states (Minnesota excepted). This should give analysts immediate pause about what social capital is and what it meant during the last half of the twentieth century and before that. Surprisingly, however, social capital (and political culture) arguments scarcely take note of such basic information. But if states with these unique and uncommon traits are the major exemplars of the social capital thesis, then that thesis is on shaky footing and would seem to have limited theoretical reach.

Also, these states with higher social capital have had lower rates of population growth over the last several decades. Data indicate that Nevada is quite low in social capital compared to most states; yet it is among the fastest-growing states while states with high social capital have been growing slowly. Is this indicative of a cause or consequence of changes in social capital? Does this imply that Americans increasingly spurn a civic orientation and supportive environments or that social capital (as understood in *BA*) can be formed and maintained only under specific and rather limited social and racial conditions? And what does this all mean for broader assumptions about social capital and prescriptions for its revival?

Within extremely homogeneous states, where social capital is found to be highest, bridging activities will (virtually by definition) be limited to those of similar racial backgrounds. Likewise, the bonding that occurs is going to be racially exclusive. Hence what typically results is bounded bridging and biased bonding. Social scientists have long noted that rational behavior is more limited, (i.e., "bounded") by various limitations of cognition, understanding, and so forth than is often assumed. Social capital may be a factor that bounds as often as it expands understanding.

For all its strengths and appeal, then, social capital analyses probably overstate some points, understate others, and misstate still others because of (a) how it conceptualizes (or fails to conceptualize) and measures social outcomes and certain elements of American society and (b) its neglect of a considerable body of American politics research. Bringing these factors into discussions of social capital yields a more realistic civic republicanism that contrasts with the "romantic" version evident in *BA* and similar works.

SUMMARY AND CONCLUSION

The social capital thesis has, in various versions, captivated many scholars of American politics and has appealed to many intellectuals because it seems intuitively accurate, is consistent with common understandings, and provides a comforting portrayal. Furthermore, a solid empirical base supporting its arguments dates back several decades (cf. Elazar 1966, 1972) and has been reaffirmed over time, according to some. *Bowling Alone* is the most recent iteration; it is the culmination of the social capital thesis, bearing the most elaborate articulation of its ideas and a massive data base. Social capital is an impressive construct, since arguably it affects many social outcomes as well as economic and social equality.

Recall that "kids are better off," "schools work better," and "health is better" in high-social capital states, which also feature greater economic and civic equality. Considerable research in this tradition has reinforced such claims, including Elazar's (1984) political culture argument and a host of later studies (cf. Gray 1999). However, some researchers have added qualifications, for example, the finding that "social connectedness" is not related to government performance (Knack 2002), and others find no support for the claims asserting social capital's beneficial impacts (Hill and Matsubayashi 2005). Most dramatically, perhaps, some argue that high social capital among blacks emerged in large part as a defensive mechanism against white prejudice and discrimination. However, even considerable amounts of social capital have not proved sufficient in such cases to achieve desired social outcomes and substantive equality (Orr 1999).

On the whole, various social capital, political culture, and civic culture arguments – which share strong similarities and come to broadly similar conclusions – appear to have a blind spot in that their civic republican orientations understate the role of race and of ascriptive hierarchy in America (Smith 1993). This highlights the need for a more direct and systematic analysis of racial diversity that can advance an argument incorporating the legacies of the philosophical tradition of inegalitarianism – in particular, racial inegalitarianism, racial hierarchy, and two-tiered pluralism (Hero 1992). This argument is pursued in the next chapter.

3

The Racial Diversity Thesis

Race and racial diversity have historically been important social forces in the American political system. The especially unique experience of blacks has long been recognized, and the distinct situations of Latinos and other minorities has come to be acknowledged in much research. But some prominent empirical theories and analyses of American politics have given little attention to the significance of such groups or to the normative philosophical traditions that support the unequal status of these groups (King and Smith 2005). The "racial diversity interpretation," in contrast, brings close theoretical attention to factors and issues explaining inegalitarianism, placing racial/ethnic diversity at the forefront of analysis. While not alone in this emphasis, it differs from other approaches in systematically stressing the general (not just regional) impacts of race, its importance in both relative and aggregate terms, and its relevance for a broad array of political dimensions. At the same time it has carefully considered other analytical traditions and approaches (Hero 1998).

The situations of various racial minority groups are, to be sure, each quite complex. For instance, the black/African American population has internal class differentiation (Hochschild 1995) and includes increasing numbers of immigrants from the

West Indies. The group referred to as "Latinos" or "Hispanics" is a diverse one, differentiated by nationality (Mexican American, Puerto Rican, Cuban, etc.), time and circumstances of entry into the United States, and a host of other factors. Similarly, Asian groups have complex and varied historical experiences in the United States. (Also, it is sometimes analytically useful to differentiate between Western and non–Western European populations when thinking about race/ethnicity in the United States. However, here I will de-emphasize the white ethnic distinction because scholarly research has suggested there are fundamentally important differences between minority groups and white ethnic immigrants, historically and currently; see Jacobson 1998; Guglielmo 2003; Hero 1992). The assumption, at least for present purposes, is that there is enough difference group situations and enough similarity across the minority groups to support the designations and arguments made (cf. Hero 1992, ch. 11). But future racial diversity analyses, on their own and in relation to other approaches, will need to be conscientious – and reformulated accordingly – in order to assess the increasing and evolving complexity of racial diversity (see Hawes et al. 2006).

The racial (or minority) diversity thesis contends that a central feature of American politics is its racial and ethnic diversity and that this diversity, or relative lack thereof, is especially evident in the population of the American states. Racial diversity entails black (African American), Latino, and other minority populations. These groups are commonly thought of as "minority groups" or "protected classes," implying unique historical experiences in the United States. The size of these racial minority populations in a state is taken as a reasonable barometer of the extent to which the legacy and current effects of racial (ascriptive) hierarchy is manifest in political jurisdictions. That is, to the extent that a state has a high concentration of minority groups, we expect to see more manifestations of historical formal (and informal) inequality. Such manifestations would include different political behaviors among minority and majority populations as well as differences in social and public policy outcomes in both absolute and relative terms (Hero 1998) – that is, outcomes having different forms or "faces." A group of large size may be viewed as a racial threat, leading to reactions from whites and, in turn, responses from minorities. Whether the reactions are based on "old-fashioned" or "symbolic" racism, group competition, social dominance, or some combination of these or other attitudes (see Chapter 7) is not always easy to ascertain in macro-level studies such as this. However, even when a racial group's size is small, outcomes indicative of a general racial hierarchy are common. That being said, a larger racial group size may sometimes lead to some political "clout" for such groups (as will be seen in later analysis).

There are states with relatively few minorities, while a number of other states have much larger proportions. (There are also differences in the distribution of "white ethnics," such as Southern or Eastern European populations.) These patterns collectively produce overall racial configurations that differ considerably across the states. Levels of diversity are an important aspect of *all* states' politics, although this importance takes different forms in different contexts. Various contexts are associated with different types of politics and policy (Hero 1998), but the American dilemma of race is reflected in some way in all the states. These comments about the importance of diversity as an interpretation are consistent with Smith's (1993, 1997) broader assertions that theories of politics in the United States should be reconsidered because so far they have neither adequately recognized nor incorporated the inegalitarian ideologies and institutions that have defined the status of racial and ethnic minorities. That is, the legacy of hierarchical and inegalitarian views – not just the civic republican and liberal – traditions are evident in American political thought and practice. However, the racial diversity thesis goes further than the multiple traditions thesis by specifying relevant indicators and then suggesting how (as well as how much) those traditions matter in contemporary society and politics. The diversity thesis contends that patterns of behavior and social and political outcomes are correlated to a considerable degree with the distribution of racial/ethnic groups in state populations.

State diversity patterns have been measured, and indicators derived from those data are used in the analyses that follow. The states fall into several groups based on their patterns of ethnic diversity. For convenience I often refer to the states in terms of these patterns or characterizations, but note that these broad categories may not convey the full complexity and nuance of state population configurations.

Compared to overall U.S. patterns, some states can be characterized as racially *homogeneous*. These states have populations that are primarily white or Anglo – that is, of Northern and Western European descent – and have small minority (black and Latino) populations and relatively few "white ethnics" (i.e., non–Northern and non–Western European whites). Some states have *bifurcated* racial structures: large minority populations, primarily black and/or Latino; a large white (nonethnic) population, and a rather small proportion of "white ethnics." Those states with average-sized minority populations and larger-than-average white ethnic populations are here referred to as *heterogeneous*.

Thus we have three state profiles: homogeneous states and two types of nonhomogeneous states, bifurcated and heterogeneous. A state fits one of these profiles based on the type and degree of its racial/ethnic diversity. But beyond merely categorizing states, considering the impact of racial contexts is important. V. O. Key's landmark *Southern Politics* (1949) and other works have "understood that people behaved differently in different contexts"; "individuals make choices among alternatives that are often shaped by their context." The central contextual factor that Key focused on was the racial composition – especially the size of the black population – of counties and states in the South during the mid-twentieth century. The diversity thesis is consistent with and expands on this theoretical tradition, suggesting that race is salient throughout the United States (albeit in different ways).

THE RACIAL DIVERSITY INTERPRETATION
AND POLITICS IN THE STATES

Given that states vary considerably in their racial "differentiation" or racial/minority diversity, what are the social and political patterns and what politics and policies are associated with them? The diversity perspective focuses attention on these and related questions, and it suggests answers based on a contextual framework. In this section I briefly recount general arguments of the diversity perspective regarding certain aspects of politics and public policy in the states (cf. Hero 1998).

The degree and types of racial diversity appear to produce general differences in the forms of political pluralism of states. In homogeneous states a "consensual pluralism" is anticipated (Putnam 2000; Elazar 1984). The diversity perspective suggests that shared or common interest is more likely where individuals are more ethnically alike and in more homogeneous contexts; shared principles are more likely where there are shared racial characteristics. A bifurcated environment, with a large minority and a large white (but small "white ethnic") population leads to a hierarchical or limited political pluralism, historically manifested in various legal and political constraints. Despite major social and political change during the most recent generation, this condition continues, though in modified form. In more heterogeneous states a "competitive pluralism" – competition between many groups, including ethnic/racial groups – is fostered by greater (white) ethnic and moderate to high minority diversity, and this condition is probably heightened by greater urbanization and other factors such as population density.

The diversity thesis has suggested that the political differences and debates that occur in homogeneous environments may be vigorous but are also something like a "family feud." High levels of engagement, which stem from issue-based, policy-oriented discussions relevant to civic virtue concerns, may arise more frequently in these than in other settings (Elazar 1984; Dye 1984). But as family feuds, the discussions are tempered because they are underpinned by social trust and a sense of reciprocity; this substantial consensus is itself grounded in broad racial similarity, according to the diversity thesis (see also Theiss-Morse and Hibbing 2005 and Chapter 7 herein). Major sources of political and social cleavage, such as deep-seated racial division that have marked much of American history, are largely absent in (white) homogeneous settings. From the standpoint of the diversity argument, then, it is important not only that serious civic engagement occurs but also that deliberations occur within a homogeneous setting. What might appear to be individualistic or interest-oriented inclinations in some contexts may more readily coincide with communal or public concerns in homogeneous settings – a result of that very social homogeneity (Hero 1998).

The diversity thesis also contends that, in homogeneous contexts, core values are widely shared even though political debates may occur about applications of values. There is agreement on basic values, and political, economic, and social equality are parts of that basic value structure and serve to reinforce it. There may be disagreement on the "means" – that is, on the interpretation and application of values – but because the stakes are not particularly vivid or potentially redistributive in racial terms, the nature of the discussion is different and appears more oriented to community or the commonwealth. In contrast, in racially bifurcated contexts there is likely to be considerable agreement, at least among the white majority, on both means (instrumental values) and ends (basic or substantive values). Such basic values are legacies of dominant group beliefs of hierarchy and how to maintain them, and racial political inequality continues.

In the in-between, heterogeneous environments, core values themselves are more open to debate because the stakes are more pronounced racially. As a result, many issues that may be viewed as relatively neutral or technocratic in the homogeneous environment become "political" issues, such as "who gets the government jobs." In the heterogeneous context there is some disagreement on both means and ends.

The diversity thesis suggests that social context is related to means to social order, social control, or "social production" (Stone 1989) in society. Consistent with other scholarship, the diversity view argues that there are several major approaches to achieving social order: community, hierarchy, and contract/market. In the U.S. political system the contract/market approach, which is based on liberal and capitalist values, is the dominant but not the only means to social order. Numerous works have been written discussing how the U.S. Constitution was influenced by the liberal tradition and social contract thought, and how the Constitution was written to support a "commercial republic" (Hartz 1955; Lowi and Ginsberg 1990; Smith 1997). The diversity thesis acknowledges that contract/market orientations are critical influences but, more significantly for present purposes, it also argues that such influence is importantly affected by the context of racial diversity. Some contexts may permit or encourage "going beyond" contract/market and individualistic orientations, prominently complementing them – as in the homogeneous context – with communal or community orientations. Other contexts – specifically, the bifurcated – have included major elements of "hierarchy," thus historically practicing egalitarian or contract traditions to a lesser degree and applying them across groups to a lesser extent than in other contexts. There is also a certain sense of community in the bifurcated context but it is rooted in hierarchical and inegalitarian assumptions; we can summarize this as "a place for everyone, and [but] everyone in their place" (Hero 1998).

RACIAL DIVERSITY: RESEARCH AND FINDINGS

Complementing the broader propositions just delineated, previous research indicates that there is extensive support for the racial diversity interpretation (Hero 1998). Racial diversity accounts for substantial variation in major state policy, including policies (or dimensions of policies) that particularly affect racial minority groups. Each contextual configuration seems to be associated with different faces of power or inequality. In the aggregate, it has been shown that the more homogeneous states have better aggregate outcomes (and this is echoed in social capital findings); at the same time, greater racial diversity (bifurcation) was associated with worse aggregate outcomes. On the whole, then, states with larger minority populations have lower social conditions while states with little diversity (homogeneous states) have the best outcomes. However, when outcomes are *dis*aggregated to consider their effects on ethnic groups, outcomes for minorities tend to be relatively low in homogeneous contexts (Hero 1998). These findings are certainly not consistent with social capital arguments.

Earlier diversity research (Hero 1998) arrived at these findings even when also explicitly taking into consideration states' political culture (Elazar 1984) – a clear precursor to and close cousin of social capital (cf. Putnam 2000, pp. 346–7) – as well as an array of other factors such as states' political ideology orientations and socioeconomic conditions (e.g., levels of education and income). Thus diversity was examined and juxtaposed to political culture, and diversity was clearly and consistently a stronger statistical predictor of outcomes for racial minorities.

Diversity is also associated with political processes, such as electoral patterns, party systems and the strength of interest-group systems. The processes examined included how strongly the right to vote was protected historically, levels of voter turnout, the extent of competition between political parties, indicators of overall democratization, the social bases of political parties' composition (i.e., class and race), the general (or "mean"/average) level of ideology (i.e., self-description as liberal or conservative and the ideological patterns of party elites); the nature of state party systems (whether the parties's orientations are more "pragmatic" or more "responsible"), and the strength of state interest-group systems (cf. Hero 1998, chs. 3 and 7).

Much less variation remains in the "right to vote" in the United States today than there once was, largely because federal legislation has assured that right and brought considerable uniformity. But research examining the difference that still existed in the 1980s and 1990s indicated that high racial diversity was associated with weaker assurances regarding a right to vote (especially in the South) whereas low social diversity was associated with stronger ease and assurance (see Hero, Tolbert, and King 2006). These patterns are hardly surprising and are reminders of the legacy of institutions and traditions typically associated with high racial diversity, particularly large black populations. Greater minority diversity is significantly related to lower voter turnout and also has a significant negative relationship to certain indicators of party competition (Hero 1998; Holbrook and Van Dunk 1993). When the racial diversity measures were considered relative to an indicator of "overall democracy" in the states, minority diversity was found to be significantly and negatively related.

Other important impacts of racial context on party patterns have been identified by Giles and Hertz (1994). In a study of Louisiana parishes they found that, as the size of black population increased (i.e., where "racial threat" was higher), there was a significantly stronger tendency of whites to join the Republican Party. Similarly, Brown (1995) found that political party affiliation in the states was appreciably affected by states 'racial composition (Hero 1998, ch. 3). Thus, race may structure political parties and party affiliation at the state level – and beyond the state level as well, according to Frymer (2005; see also Carmines and Stimson 1989). More minority diversity is also related to more powerful interest-group systems in the states; stronger interest-group systems have been found to consistently favor the "haves" over the "have-nots," and minority groups are concentrated among the latter. Furthermore, groups directly representing minority interests are not among the powerful interest groups in the states; indeed, such groups are seldom seen as at all influential (Hero 1998).

"Descriptive representation" – the extent to which the proportions of a group in a political jurisdiction are more similar to proportions of the group within a governmental body (here, the congruence of minority population proportions in general compared to their proportions in state legislatures and state bureaucracies) – is quite strongly associated with racial diversity. Generally, larger minority population overall is associated with increased underrepresentation. But an especially interesting finding was that some of the most homogeneous states had the largest underrepresentation of minorities in their state bureaucracies (Hero 1998, ch. 4).

Racial diversity also appeared to have effects on several major policy outcomes in the states: education, welfare, and health. Evidence from the early to mid-1980s had found that social diversity is related to education (graduation and student suspensions) and to health (infant mortality) policies. Especially notable was that racial diversity often had an impact on aggregate patterns as well as on disaggregated ("differential") patterns, i.e., outcomes for minority populations relative to general outcomes (Hero and Tolbert 1996). When these and other related policies were reassessed with evidence from the 1990s, the further examination supported to a substantial degree the earlier findings relative to policy outcomes, and other notable findings also emerged (Hero 1998).

Greater minority diversity was related to better *relative* outcomes such as higher black graduation ratios and lower minority suspension ratios, while some of the worst relative outcomes were found in homogeneous states (which have high social capital and tend to be moralistic). Minority diversity has a significant impact both on overall infant mortality rates (positive effect) and on minority/overall rates (negative effect). That is, more minority diversity is related to higher overall (worse) infant mortality rates but also to better differential ratios. A number of these relationships echo those of earlier studies, suggesting that diversity has significant implications for these issues and that this has been the case for some time. Diversity was examined relative to an array of other policies. Perhaps most significantly, racial diversity was found to be strongly related to a major criminal justice issue, incarceration rates, for the 1980s and the early 1990s. More minority diversity is associated with relatively less disparate incarceration rates for minorities; and some of the more homogeneous states (e.g., Minnesota and Iowa) had among the most disparate outcomes. Again, the patterns are consistent with findings from the early 1980s and thus do not appear to be temporally isolated.

Research has found that minority diversity was related to the adoption of "official English" policies in the states during the late 1980s. Later adoptions of such policies in the mid-1990s in several relatively homogeneous states follow a pattern found a number of times in this study: the homogeneous and bifurcated settings stand out in terms of various policy outcomes, although in different ways. Responses to diversity are pronounced in relative or absolute terms in each of these two settings. Overall, diversity is shown to shape public policies, especially certain aspects of education, health, and criminal justice policies (Hawes et al. 2006; see also Chapter 4 herein).

In addition to the considerable body just summarized of research self-consciously associated with the racial diversity thesis per se, there is abundant research documenting the importance of race in American politics; however, much of this latter body of research has not directly engaged or been juxtaposed to the social capital or related arguments. Much of the research highlighting the importance of race examines periods during the height of social capital in the United States and/or coincident with the decline of social capital, but most of this research has not confronted the social capital thesis directly.

One study in the urban arena did examine blacks and their levels of social capital. It found that blacks have been relatively *un*successful in shaping education reform in Baltimore despite having substantial amounts of social capital (Orr 1999). In short, there is ample evidence that race has been an important factor in explaining various outcomes in American state (and local) government. Additional evidence supports this.

Race and Welfare Policy

A substantial body of scholarship has demonstrated that race fundamentally shaped the broad design and evolution of the American welfare state. Ward (2005) argues that, during the Progressive Era, Mothers' Pensions were premised on a policy of racial discrimination against blacks and other minorities, including immigrants. An important program in its own right, the Mothers' Pensions were also precursors to later programs that formed the core of what became the key elements of the American welfare state: Aid to Dependent Children (ADC) in the 1930s, renamed Aid to Families with Dependent Children (AFDC) in the 1950s. Lieberman (2003) makes the case that racial considerations affected welfare policy, emphasizing that blacks and other minorities constituted especially high proportions of workers in certain occupations – such as maids, farmers and migrant workers – that were excluded from coverage under the original welfare legislation in 1935. Echoing Lieberman and adding to this line of argument, Katznelson (2005) has shown that blacks benefited substantially less than others from Depression-era and later social policies such as labor legislation and the GI Bill. On the whole, social security and welfare policies were constrained in their formulation and typically much more so in their administration through a decentralized system that gave states and localities much discretion in the implementation process. As a result, benefits accruing to blacks did indeed occur, but the *gaps* between whites and blacks often increased after adoption of these policies (Katznelson 2005, pp. 140–1; also see King and Smith 2005).

Even with (and arguably because of) the expansion of welfare policy in the 1960s, which also coincided with civil rights
and voting rights legislation, racial overtones regarding welfare
policy became more apparent in popular discourse over time.
According to Gilens (2003), until the 1960s "poverty appeared
overwhelmingly as a 'white problem'" in the American news
media. But "beginning in 1965, the media's portrayal of American poverty shifted dramatically. Although the true racial composition of the American poor remained stable, the face of
poverty in the news media became markedly darker between
1965 and 1967." Gilens attributes these changing perceptions to
several developments. Massive black migration from the South
to the North, particularly prevalent from the 1940s to the 1960s,
was an "initial link in a chain of events that led to the dramatic
changes in how Americans thought about poverty." Between
1940 and 1970 the proportion of blacks among welfare (AFDC)
recipients grew steadily, and "as the welfare rolls expanded
sharply in the 1960s and 1970s, the American public's attention was drawn disproportionately to poor blacks." Against
this backdrop, the "more proximate events" leading to major
changes in Americans' views of the poor "were a shift in the focus
within the civil rights movement from the fight for legal equality to the battle for economic equality, and the urban riots that
rocked [America] during the summers of 1964 through 1968"
(Gilens 2003). Greater black participation in welfare programs,
together with blacks' quest for not only equal opportunity but
also equal outcomes, profoundly affected popular views of "the
most conspicuous program [AFDC] to aid the poor." Although
the early formulation of the American welfare state substantially limited the participation of blacks (Lieberman 2003), the
extent of their benefits from the later American welfare state
were exaggerated, resulting in distorted perceptions of their presence among welfare recipients (Gilens 2003). Welfare and race
became increasingly conflated in the public mind, with attendant
implications. Note that the time frame Gilens specifies coincides
with the decline of social capital as described by Putnam.

A sizable body of research attests to the significance of race for welfare policy in the American states, with larger racial minority group presence being associated with less extensive welfare policies. In one study, Johnson (2001) examined states' "average AFDC payment per recipient" in 1990 and found that racial diversity in states has a direct influence on those payments; that is, as racial diversity increases, welfare payments decrease. Racial diversity also had an indirect influence, shaping the racial attitudes of the majority group (whites). Aid to Families with Dependent Children was in place with relatively modest changes from 1935 until the Welfare Reform Act of 1996; thus, in his analysis Johnson (2001) evaluated welfare policy before the reform. Later, Johnson (2003) examined the post–welfare reform period, and his earlier findings of a negative impact of racial diversity – higher percentages of black welfare recipients correlated with lower average monthly welfare benefits – were reaffirmed. Johnson concludes: "it appears that policymakers have a different relationship with the racial majority in their states than with the racial minority: They *respond* to whites and *react* to the presence of African Americans" (2003, pp. 161–3, emphasis in original).

Other analyses of welfare policy in the post-reform period, when TANF (Temporary Assistance for Needy Families) block grants replaced AFDC, further underscore the impact of race in the formulation and implementation of welfare policy. Soss et al. (2001) found that higher percentages of African Americans on state welfare rolls were related to stricter sanctions, stricter time limits, and family caps. In addition, states with higher percentages of Latino recipients tended to have stricter time limits and family caps. Higher percentages of the two groups also tended to affect benefit levels negatively. In short, race/ethnicity was consistently associated with the various welfare policies examined; in the researchers' words, *"the 'problem of the color line' remains central* to American welfare politics" (Soss et al. 2001, pp. 385–91, emphasis added). Yet another analysis (Fellowes and Rowe 2004) confirms these earlier findings regarding "the strong role of race in TANF politics," as evidenced in three dimensions of the policy. A higher percentage of African American recipients leads to: (i) *stricter rules* governing initial eligibility, (ii) *less flexibility* in new welfare work requirements, and (iii) *lower cash benefits* to welfare recipients. Fellowes and Rowe also found a negative relationship between the percentage of welfare recipients who are Latino and cash benefit levels, indicating that the racialization of welfare is not limited to black populations.

Finally, the analysis of Keiser, Mueser, and Choi (2004) focuses on the implementation of TANF policy through a case study of Missouri. This state has an African American population that is slightly larger than the national average proportion, and Missouri's "sanction policy is administratively similar to other states in the level of discretion given" to bureaucrats responsible for direct implementation. This analysis of sanctions (i.e., "a reduction in the case grant for recipients failing to meet training, work, or other requirements") finds that "sanction rates increase as the nonwhite population increases." This pattern does change, however, when blacks reach a majority of the population. This study of post-reform welfare policy implementation further highlights the importance of race, but none of these welfare studies considers the social capital factor.

Diversity and the Adoption of Direct Democracy

Racial and ethnic factors also appear central to understanding the historical patterns of the adoption and contemporary use of the initiative and referendum as institutional practices in the states. These practices of "direct democracy" have come to play a prominent role in contemporary policy making. The presence of direct democracy processes increase overall political participation in the states, but they have frequently been used to blunt or reverse policies favored by racial and ethnic groups, such as affirmative action and bilingual education. The adoption and use of direct democracy in states as racially different today (though formerly much less so) as North Dakota and California are phenomena that invite consideration and discussion.

Schmidt (1989) argues that differences in racial/ethnic diversity in the West and the South in the early twentieth century are central to understanding why the initiative practice was commonly adopted in the former but not in the latter states during the Progressive Era. Part of the reason that western states were among the most likely to adopt the initiative was that "the majority of residents in the boom towns of the West were *white native U.S.* citizens who had moved in from other states, *not other countries*, and therefore *did not represent the same kind of threat*" as blacks and immigrants did in other parts of the United States (Schmidt 1989, p. 13, emphases added). It was "not that westerners were not racist – it was simply that the victims of western racism were not numerous enough to outvote the native U.S. citizens," according to Schmidt. In contrast with the self-reliant egalitarianism of the West, "southern politics was still steeped in aristocratic – and racist – traditions." Furthermore, Schmidt shows that resistance to the initiative in the South was related to fears of Negro influence. Memories of Reconstruction were such that concerns over the possibility that blacks might regain political influence stifled support for the initiative. Schmidt's claims and reasoning are affirmed by another, later study.

Using an event history framework, Bowler, Donovan, and Lawrence (2005) examined the adoption of the initiative and referendum mechanisms in the states. They found that higher percentages of nonwhites and Roman Catholics in states "decreased the likelihood" of adopting direct democracy. Furthermore, Bowler et al. emphatically reject the claim that this impact of nonwhites was due solely to nonadoption in southern states, because their basic findings remain when those states are removed from the statistical analysis. Overall, then, the historical record strongly suggests that racial factors have affected the (non)adoption of "direct democracy." But other ethnic factors – the size of white ethnic populations – has also affected institutions in the states.

Schmidt suggests that a major "factor that hindered the establishment of I&R [the initiative and referendum] in the Northeast was the high proportion of immigrants in the cities." Most of the immigrants, from "southern and eastern Europe," were poorer and less educated than their "northern European predecessors" and the "political differences between the two groups were immense." "White Anglo-Saxon Protestants feared the immigrants' potential voting power and doubted their ability to read, much less comprehend, ballot questions" (Schmidt 1989). Also, Schmidt suggests that racism and related factors influenced the adoption of the initiative. Schmidt speaks of the "tendency of rural white politicians in the East and South [in the early 1900s] to oppose I&R, fearing that the urban masses, once empowered by I&R, would overrule the decisions of malapportioned legislatures dominated by rural interests." Thus, a frequent pattern was that state legislatures in these regions allowed the initiative in cities "but not statewide."

The point is that racial and ethnic considerations have influenced the very structure of state political systems for many years. That is, the highest levels of social capital occurred within an institutional environment that was importantly shaped by race. It has also been found that Hispanics, the largest minority group in California, have consistently been the biggest losers on ballot initiatives (devices of direct democracy) related to racial issues in that state in the 1980s and 1990s (Hajnal, Gerber, and Louch 2002; Tolbert and Grummel 2003).

There are additional cases where importance of race for other institutions and practices in American politics can be identified. Frymer makes a powerful argument that the larger structure and processes of the American political party system have discouraged responsiveness to black and other racial concerns. Political parties are major mediating institutions: they are situated at the intersection between the public in general and governing institutions that serve to educate citizens about political processes, socialize the public about civic duties, and mobilize people into political activity and involvement (Wolbrecht 2005). Scholars have commonly held a positive view of the way political parties and the two-party system presumably facilitate the recognition of minorities in the political process. But Frymer (2005) contends that many basic aspects of the political system were created in a way that sought to dissipate and avoid fundamental conflicts over race (see also Wolbrecht 2005, pp. 104–5). The median voter is particularly important in political parties' quest to win elections, and in the American two-party system the median voter is especially pivotal. Despite (or perhaps because of) America's historical legacy of race, the median voter tends not to be highly concerned about – and is often unsympathetic to – policies aimed at improving the situation of racial/ethnic minorities, according to Frymer (2005; cf. Hochschild 1995). Hence, it is argued that both the Democrat and Republican parties have little incentive to take on relevant policy issues because this might fracture their electoral coalitions. Given the critical role of parties in connecting citizens to government and in stimulating civic engagement and political participation, Frymer's thesis is especially telling.

Racial factors have been shown to shape other institutions of American government. King and Smith (2005) demonstrate how the structure and workings of the U.S. Congress and federal bureaucracy was for decades part of the American "racial order" that played a major role in maintaining white supremacy. Burns's (1994) study of the formation of local governments indicates that the very creation and the physical boundaries of those governments frequently had racial overtones and subsequent racial implications. To the extent that formal governmental boundaries shape, foster, and perhaps even institutionalize social interaction, civic engagement, political participation, and policy agendas,

Burns's findings are relevant not only to race but also the claims of social capital theorists. (cf. Jones-Correa 2000).

Summary

There are a number of important findings and insights of the diversity interpretation. Racial diversity contexts seem to have broad effects, to shape general notions of social order, and to have significance for an array of issues in state politics and policy. Racial diversity helps account for political and policy variation with respect to specific racial impacts of policies, not only in the aggregate. Numerous studies (including social capital studies) concerning social outcomes and race address the aggregate issues but do not concern themselves with specific racial effects, especially the dynamics of race and ethnicity in homogeneous contexts. The direct acknowledgment of and ability to address several dimensions of state policy is distinctive of the racial diversity thesis. Racial diversity – and the way this perspective has been applied – thus adds appreciably to our understanding of politics by being more theoretically inclusive and complete than other analytic approaches. When considered systematically, racial diversity recasts the study and understanding of American politics.

Moreover, many studies seem to imply that race is primarily relevant to explaining politics in the southern states and in other selected circumstances, often examining states by separating the South and non-South. However, the relevance of race beyond this distinction is seldom developed (Bowler et al. 2005). Diversity research, in contrast, provides evidence that when politics and policies are analyzed more closely and are disaggregated – that is, when politics and outcomes are examined in both relative and in absolute terms – racial and ethnic factors often become more apparent and their implications are more significant in all types of population profiles. The evidence suggests that there are several faces of politics and inequality that are substantially related to diversity. A frequent finding is that states that do well in absolute terms do poorly in relative terms this is characteristic of homogeneous states. On the other hand, in states with high racial diversity (bifurcated), the situation is usually reversed. Thus, racial and ethnic factors are important for understanding politics and policy in all of the states, not just in one region or set of states nor with respect to only a few issues.

The core claim, which is supported with extensive evidence, is that racial diversity is a significant aspect of state politics that is substantially greater, more pervasive, and more institutional in its importance than has been sufficiently acknowledged or understood by other analytical approaches. As such, diversity can reasonably be thought of as an analytical construct and not "just another" variable, because it is a phenomenon that is imbedded in the U.S. political system and that represents a distinct perspective on American politics (King and Smith 2005).

Each type of diversity (especially homogeneity and bifurcation) seems to be associated with different patterns of inequality. Diversity patterns form different contexts, and diversity's significance is evident across contexts but in different forms, with the particular forms being influenced by specific racial contexts. The extent to which this holds also in homogeneous settings is an especially interesting finding.

Most state politics research focuses primarily, or solely, on aggregate indicators – on the "levels" or "quantity" or "quality" of policies, which may be thought of as one face of politics. But there are other faces. That concerning the distributive consequences of state policy is another, one that is often overlooked in research designs of most mainstream studies. Here, the policy patterns are often rather different than in the first face. These other dimensions are no less substantive than those of the first but are too often ignored. The diversity interpretation not only brings attention to these other faces, it also helps explain them. In addition, the findings suggest that if we think of policies as "institutions" (Pierson 1994, pp. 42–5), then racial diversity is a particularly important social force in state politics with major implications for U.S. politics generally.

Diversity's relevance at another level of the political system, the "substate" level, has been explored with regard to voting patterns and political attitudes on several questions as well as substate institutions (Orr 1999 Hero 1998, ch. 7). There have been several notable studies that have demonstrated the implications of racial context for individuals' political attitudes. Some research has shown that both racial "threat" and racial "isolation" may be related to negative attitudes toward minorities; it appears that isolation or insulation may beget insularity (Link and Oldendick 1996). Studies of states' county-level voting patterns on ballot initiatives also suggest that racial diversity has an impact (Tolbert and Hero 1996); its influence seems most pronounced in bifurcated and in homogeneous contexts – again, not unlike patterns found in earlier analyses. Third, studies of county-level voting patterns in state candidate-based elections, and over extended periods of time, indicate the importance of counties' racial/minority composition in a number of states (Gimpel 1996). Taken individually and collectively, the numerous pieces of evidence strongly point to the importance of racial diversity at the substate level (Hero 1998, ch. 7; Soss, Langbein, and Metelko 2003).

The evidence supporting the diversity thesis is considerable (Hero 1998; see also other evidence noted earlier in this chapter). When examined in the aggregate, more diversity is related to worse social outcomes. This also reflects the lower or disadvantaged economic and political status of minority groups, which may be perceived as a racial threat (Key 1949; Giles and Hertz 1994) and create backlash effects (Radcliff and Saiz 1995). Low diversity (homogeneity) is associated with better overall outcomes because of the diminished presence of these socially disadvantaged groups, which also implies that they are less threatening.

When examined in relative or differential terms, racial minorities often do relatively well (compared to whites) in more diverse settings than they do in more homogeneous settings. It should be noted that minorities' situations are still unequal in high-diversity (bifurcated) contexts, but they are at least somewhat less so than in more homogeneous contexts. It appears that if minority populations become sufficiently large then they can – through political mobilization and representation – mitigate (though not eliminate) the extent of inequality (Hero 1998; Orr 1999; Meier and Stewart 1991; Keiser et al. 2004). Minorities' ability to mobilize and achieve formal representation was facilitated by the civil rights legislation and related legislation of the mid-1960s.

RACIAL DIVERSITY'S CONCEPTUAL CHALLENGE TO SOCIAL CAPITAL

Later chapters provide extensive empirical evidence juxtaposing the racial diversity and social capital arguments. For the moment it is useful to initially suggest how the diversity thesis differs from and challenges the social capital thesis.

Evidence supporting the racial diversity thesis was found in earlier studies (Hero 1998) even after accounting for a number of other factors, including states' ideology, socioeconomic characteristics, various political traits, and – most importantly for present purposes – Elazar's political culture measures. In virtually every instance, when the diversity and the political culture measures were examined jointly (along with other factors) the importance of diversity clearly outweighed that of political culture. Because political culture can be seen as a predecessor and close relative of social capital, there are plausible reasons to think that comparing diversity and social capital will yield analogous results. (This is empirically demonstrated in the next chapter.)

The social capital thesis (and related arguments) essentially overlooks the role of race in American history and politics; and even when the importance of race is forcefully acknowledged, it is not fully or appropriately incorporated into the empirical analysis. Specifically, social capital studies focus on overall outcomes and indicators; they do not disaggregate data in a way that permits analysis of relative, racially specific effects. As with the social capital measure itself, the dependent variables (i.e., the "outcome" measures examined) do not take race into account. "Racial composition" is often examined as a secondary *in*dependent variable, but all of the outcome indicators are aggregate or overall rates; none are ratios designed to consider – and thus obviously cannot tap into – relative or differential outcomes for racial/ethnic groups (cf. Meier and Stewart 1991; Hero 1998; Hero and Tolbert 1996). Racial inequality can hardly be found in social capital and political culture studies because the research design virtually assures that such influences will be difficult to discern; and attention to research that *has* addressed such concerns is also missing in many studies. Moreover, the dependent variables virtually ignore "social control" activities or outcomes such as relative incarceration patterns. Yet civil society is about social order and social control as much as about the facilitation of various social goals.

The social capital thesis is an influential perspective presented in a provocative and compelling theoretical and empirical work; it also represents a major school of thought on American politics (cf. Smith 1993; Stevens 1995). For all its strengths, however, social capital perspectives typically provide only a partial picture of American politics – owing to the particular conceptualization and related measurement of racial/ethnic dimensions of American politics as well as to the neglect of a large body of relevant American politics research. In other words, the treatment of race in America within the social capital thesis, and hence its understanding of American civil society, is incomplete. As a consequence, that study systematically understates the racial dimensions of American civil society (see Putnam 2000, p. 355).

Because social capital studies are neither designed nor inclined to gauge the impacts of race in American civic and political arenas, their findings apply primarily to the white population; thus, what is thought to be evidence supporting salutary ideas about "community" are essentially much more pertinent to some segments of society than others. However accurate social capital arguments may seem, their adequacy for a deep understanding of the politics of American equality appear questionable. I now turn to systematically juxtaposing and assessing the racial diversity and social capital theses.

4

Examining Social Outcomes,
and Civic and Economic Equality

The previous chapters presented the major theoretical arguments and associated research findings of two theoretical perspectives, racial diversity (Chapter 3) and social capital (Chapter 2). Theoretical and conceptual differences between the two were also discussed. Although they were treated as essentially separate theories, it was also implied that there is contention, interconnection, and overlap; indeed, the diversity thesis suggests that social capital is in considerable part an artifact of diversity (a notion we shall develop more fully in this chapter). What follows in this and the two succeeding chapters is a series of analyses juxtaposing the two perspectives in a variety of ways, emphasizing macro-level analyses but also bringing in some micro-level analysis. Before turning directly to those analyses, however, some preliminary discussion is essential.

I have suggested that social capital and racial diversity are interrelated and possibly in tension. To assess that with empirical evidence, I examined the relationship between the social

This chapter is a slightly revised version of a previously published article by Rodney E. Hero: "Social Capital and Racial Inequality in America," *Perspectives on Politics*, 1, 1 (March 2003): 113–122. Copyright © 2003 by the American Political Science Association. Reprinted with the permission of Cambridge University Press. It has also been supplemented with additional evidence from other research.

capital index (Putnam 2000) and minority diversity (i.e., percentage of black, Latino, and Asian population; see Hero 1998) in the states and found a rather strongly negative relationship (adjusted $r = -.58$, $R^2 = .33$ to .43, depending on whether a "squared term" is used to capture an upward swing in the regression line). This relation is illustrated in Figure 4-1. More minority diversity is related to less social capital overall; and a third or more of social capital appears to be attributable to racial/ethnic diversity. This is a telling but not especially surprising result, given the strong relationship between social capital and political culture indicated in *Bowling Alone (BA)* ($R^2 = .52$; Putnam 2000, p. 487 n. 11) and in light of the substantial statistical relationship between racial (and general social) diversity and political culture demonstrated in previous research (Hero 1998, pp. 9–14; Hero and Tolbert 1996; cf. Hero 1992). Stated in broader terms, racial diversity and social capital are intertwined and somewhat negatively interrelated. Perhaps especially interesting is that there are no states listed in the upper right quadrant of Figure 4-1, the quadrant indicating high diversity *and* high social capital. With this background, we turn to an intentionally methodical analysis of various social and economic indicators of equality. In the process of examining the various indicators, we consider issues of relative equality. Especially in the investigation of economic inequality – poverty and income – we explore how class and race intersect and whether that intersection is affected by levels of social capital.

EXAMINING SUBSTANTIVE OUTCOMES

The analysis of social outcomes is based on numerous and powerful findings regarding such issues, and it is central to – and provides the strongest evidence on behalf of – the social capital thesis. Accordingly, I begin by considering several social outcome measures that parallel some of those that *BA* uses in its analysis of the social capital thesis (Putnam 2000, chs. 16–20). As is appropriate to our focus on issues of racial inequality,

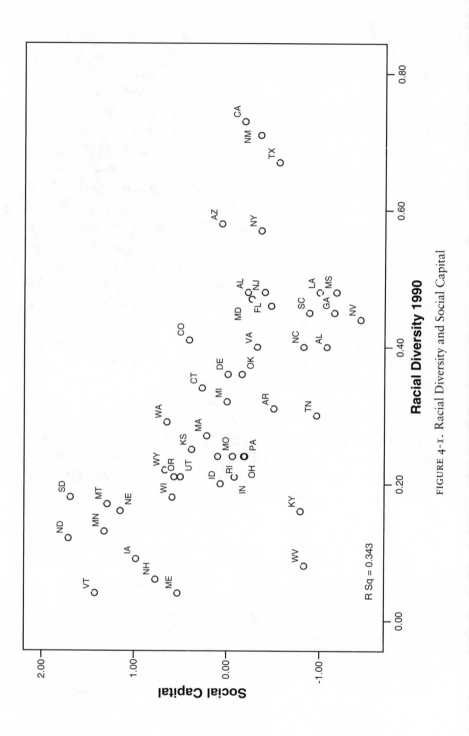

FIGURE 4-1. Racial Diversity and Social Capital

the indicators used here emphasize *differential* racial/ethnic outcomes, that is, outcome ratios measuring rates for minorities relative to (i.e., divided by) the rates for whites within a given state (cf. Meier and Stewart 1991, p. 227; Meier et al. 1989; Hero 1998). (*Rates* are percentages for the group divided by that same group's proportions in the population; *ratios* are the rate for one group divided by the rate for the other group.) Aggregate patterns may be appropriate measures for some studies and purposes. But in examining aggregate indicators – and not considering minority to white ratios or even rates – social capital studies overlook and thus mask relationships between social capital and race, including differential racial outcomes.

The social capital thesis would clearly lead to an expectation of better outcomes where there is higher social capital; indeed, this is what such analyses find. However, other research casts doubt on whether that expectation holds regarding relative minority outcomes (Meier et al. 1989; Hero 1998). I have examined social capital relative to ratio indicators of minorities on school graduation, school suspension, incarceration, and infant mortality. This was done using two methods of regression analysis as well as bivariate analysis; I also controlled for levels of minority diversity. One of the most notable patterns is the rather disparate (i.e., unequal) outcomes *generally* for minorities when relative or differential patterns are examined. The evidence is presented in Table 4-1 and will be discussed next.

Minority School Graduation Ratios

As shown in the table, there is a negative relationship between minority/white graduation rates and social capital, and this is so regardless of whether the overall level of racial diversity is accounted for. This may be surprising from the standpoint of the social capital thesis, but it is quite consistent with previous findings from social diversity analyses (Meier et al. 1989; Hero 1998, pp. 91–2).

TABLE 4-1. *Minority Outcomes Ratios and Social Capital: Regression Results*

Dependent Variables	Bivariate		Controlling for Minority Diversity	
	OLS	Robust Regression	OLS	Robust Regression
Graduation	−.0496382***	−.0780829****	−.0429675*	−.0726517****
	(.0179085)	(.0145365)	(.0222592)	(.0173287)
R^2	0.143		0.148	
Adj. R^2	0.124		0.110	
N	48	47	48	48
Suspension	.3080235****	.2823047****	.2117076**	.138985*
	(.080709)	(.0802369)	(.0975689)	(.0789548)
R^2	0.240		0.285	
Adj. R^2	0.224		0.254	
N	48	48	48	48
Incarceration	2.126751***	2.173288***	2.0681**	2.105147**
	(.7110515)	(.6696767)	(.8664932)	(.8246208)
R^2	0.165		0.166	
Adj. R^2	0.147		0.128	
N	47	47	47	47
Infant mortality	−.0705223	−.0790003	−.1579896	−.1656522
	(.1036806)	(.1107827)	(.1166358)	(.1227734)
R^2	0.012		0.071	
Adj. R^2	−0.014		0.021	
N	40	40	40	40

Note: * significant at .1 level, two-tailed test; ** significant at .05 level, two-tailed test; *** significant at .01 level, two-tailed test; **** significant at .001 level, two-tailed test. Entries are unstandardized regression coefficients with standard errors in parentheses; Adj. = Adjusted.

Minority School Suspension Ratios

When examining minority suspensions, which can be viewed as a social control or social order activity within the school environment, the relationship with social capital again indicates a worse outcome, and the relationship is stronger than for graduation ratios (cf. Hero 1998, pp. 92–3). Figure 4-2 illustrates this

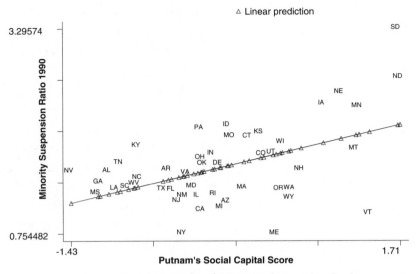

FIGURE 4-2. Social Capital and Minority Suspension Ratio

finding and also gives some sense of the patterns for other dependent variables that consider relative outcomes.

The findings on education are consistent with Meier and Stewart's thesis (1991; also see Meier et al. 1989; Hero 1998) on "second generation discrimination" in education, a thesis that seems applicable beyond education outcomes. Meier and Stewart argue that, since the formal segregation of students ended in the 1950s and 1960s (following *Brown v. Board of Education*), considerable segregation has occurred *within* schools through such practices as ability grouping ("tracking") and differential disciplinary practices and outcomes, segregation that ultimately manifests in such general outcomes as graduation and dropout rates. The findings presented here echo those of Meier and Stewart.

Minority (Black) Incarceration Ratios

Focusing on black/white incarceration patterns, there is yet again a strong relationship between social capital and black incarceration ratios – indicating clearly worse outcomes – and this occurs across all analyses including the one that controls for levels of minority diversity. ("Minority" incarceration indicators were not used because data on Hispanics are imprecise: Hispanics are included under "other," so one cannot be entirely certain what number of people in this category are Hispanic.).

The data in the statistical analysis are based on blacks, but data on incarceration (for 1993) of Native Americans were also scanned. In South Dakota, the state with second highest score on the social capital index, Native Americans constitute 23 percent of those incarcerated even though they account for only 7 percent of the state's population – that is, a 3.2:1 disparity ratio. This further undermines the assertion of better outcomes for minorities in high–social capital contexts.

Minority Infant Mortality Ratios

The relationship of social capital to minority infant mortality does not indicate worse outcomes for minorities; but neither are the outcomes any better (there is no statistically significant relationship). Nonetheless, additional information is notable. Data from the early 1980s and into the 1990s indicate that Minnesota and Iowa, the states with the fourth- and seventh-highest levels of social capital (Putnam 2000), have particularly high black infant mortality rates. Each had rates for minorities that were more than twice as high as the state's total infant mortality rate: 22.5 to 9.8 in Minnesota and 21.8 to 8.9 in Iowa. In fact, the 1990 black infant mortality rates in Minnesota and Iowa were similar to (and even slightly worse than) those for the five states *BA* indicates have the *lowest* social capital: Nevada, Mississippi, Georgia, Alabama, and Louisiana (Albritton 1990, p. 441; cf. Hero 1998).

Collectively, this evidence strongly suggests that higher social capital in a state is not associated with better relative social outcomes for racial minorities; nor is its impact simply neutral. Instead, relative outcomes for minorities are often worse in higher–social capital contexts, and this finding holds even after accounting for the size of minority populations. The numerous better overall social outcomes in high–social capital states (Putnam 2000, chs. 16–22) apparently result primarily from the outcomes for the large white (i.e., nonminority) populations in relatively homogeneous states, which contrast substantially with those of the small minority populations. One can speculate briefly about the reasons.

The patterns may arise from insular attitudes among the dominant white groups in homogeneous, racially isolated settings, as suggested in previous research (Kinder and Mendelberg 1995; Dahl 1996; Tolbert and Hero 1996). Such attitudes may be reinforced and even magnified via ostensibly neutral applications of rules and procedures that actually have disparate impacts on small minority groups. The impacts on minorities are less visible in the aggregate statistics from homogeneous settings; and minority groups are small and thus less able to mount a political challenge to the disparate outcomes. The cumulative effect of these attitudes and institutional forces are the patterns we have previously identified. But only when properly examined – when disaggregated through relative/differential indicators – is this apparent. Focusing only on aggregated rates (as do social capital studies) misses these significant outcomes.

A Note on Minority Rates

The preceding analysis emphasizes minority compared to white patterns, or *ratios*, and appropriately so. The logic of the diversity argument (cf. Meier et al. 1989; Hero 1998) – as well as the social capital thesis's emphasis on "community" and "inclusion" – implies that minorities' situation relative to that of whites *within* states is the proper one to examine. But some analysts, including some in the social capital tradition, might well contend that the proper question should be whether minorities do better in one state than in another state; that is, perhaps analysis should focus on the condition of minority groups *across* states and not only relative to their within-state nonminority counterparts. For example, do we ask whether high–social capital states have "better" incarceration rates for blacks than low–social capital states (rather than assessing the black/white patterns within states as tapped by ratio indicators)? The diversity perspective does not suppose that this is the right question to ask, but I examine it nonetheless. As will be seen, the answer to such questions are usually No, further undercutting the claims of the social capital thesis.

Analysis indicates that black incarceration rates are no better (i.e., no more equitable) where there is higher social capital. The relation between the two variables is not statistically significant one way or the other. Similarly, the relation between social capital and minority infant mortality rates are not statistically significant – that is, outcomes are no better. Suspension rates are likewise no better after controlling for minority diversity. The graduation rates for blacks (but not Latinos) *are* better as aggregate social capital increases, which strongly supports the social capital thesis. Yet perhaps even this should be qualified somewhat in light of other findings on rates and ratios of school suspensions, dropouts, and incarceration. That is, the graduation rates for minorities who remain in school are better across states, but that is not an altogether reassuring conclusion when considered in the broader context indicated by our other findings. And the issue of causal direction – what causes what – arises as well.

For only one of the four indicators, then, are *rates* better for minorities as aggregate social capital increases in a state. However, the earlier findings on *ratios* suggest that, more often than not, minorities tend to be worse-off relative to their nonminority in-state counterparts. Taken together, this evidence suggests that, if social capital's impact is examined in terms of conditions not just being "better" (overall) but "better *for whom?*" (i.e., relatively), then conclusions rather different from those of social capital studies emerge. The aggregate disparity patterns, coupled with the specific evidence on ratios and rates, strongly undermine social capital assertions (see Putnam 2000, chs. 16–22).

Examining the social capital thesis from the standpoint of minority diversity, the data indicate substantial racial/ethnic disparities on each of the measures we examine. Indeed, it is most often not a question of whether but instead of how much disparity is found – and if it varies systematically with levels of social capital. Relative outcomes for racial minorities (ratios) are no better in high–social capital settings and they may be worse. For three of the four indicators, not even minority rates are better. Social capital findings regarding social outcomes thus seem limited and applicable only to nonminority populations; the consequences of aggregate high social capital for minorities seem, if anything, detrimental. This more complete account of outcomes casts serious doubt on the essentially benign interpretation advanced in social capital studies (Putnam 2000). Subsequent research examining a similar set of outcomes casts still more doubt on the social capital thesis.

Drawing on a unique survey (from MediaMark Research Inc.), Hawes et al. (2006) developed a measure of "social capital that varies through time," unlike the static indicator of social capital used in *Bowling Alone*; furthermore, the measure Hawes et al. create correlates very strongly with Putnam's (2000) social capital index. They examined the effects of their dynamic social capital measure and of racial diversity (while controlling for a number of other variables) on school suspensions, assignment to special education classes, and infant mortality as well as on black/white and Latino/white incarceration ratios. Some of the major findings of their study are noteworthy.

Regarding the four dependent variables considered, "the social capital measure only reaches statistically significant levels for the black/white suspension and the incarceration ratio." The direction of these coefficients "is positive, indicating that *black suspension and incarceration rates (relative to white suspension rates) are higher in states with higher levels of social capital*" (Hawes et al. 2006, p. 23, emphasis added). They add that "the substantive effects are relatively weak, however." Although the effects may be modest, that only two of the four relationships are at all significant and that these two indicate that conditions for minorities are *worse* where there is higher social capital, constitutes another clear rebuke of the social capital argument and also stands in stark contrast to the powerfully "better" outcomes claimed in *BA*. The evidence on Latinos in the analysis by Hawes et al. further erodes the contentions of the social capital thesis concerning matters of racial/ ethnic equality.

Similar to the African American models, social capital is a significant predictor of the Latino/white suspension ratio, where *higher levels of social capital are associated with higher Latinos suspension rates relative to whites*. Likewise, social capital is positively and significantly related to the Latino/white special education ratio. Thus, *Latinos are expected to fare worse relative to whites in states with higher levels of social capital.* (Hawes et al. 2006, pp. 25–6, emphases added)

For Black and Latino outcomes both, Hawes et al. conclude that "the effects of diversity are relatively consistent with" previous findings of racial diversity research (e.g., Hero 1998, 2003a).

CIVIC AND ECONOMIC EQUALITY

Along with its claims about the beneficial effects of social capital on social outcomes (Putnam 2000, chs. 16–20), a particularly significant finding of social capital research concerns civic and economic equality; specifically, higher social capital is said to be strongly associated with more civic and social equality (pp. 359–61). The index of "civic equality" employed in *BA* was "based on *class* differences in rates of political participation, as measured in Roper Social and Political Trends surveys [aggregated over 1974 to 1994]. For each of the twelve forms of political participation – signing petitions, attending public meetings, and so on" – a "ratio of the logged incidence in the top quintile of the income distribution to the bottom quintile of the income distribution" was constructed (pp. 497, 359, emphasis added).

The civic equality index, like the social capital index in general, does not disaggregate according to race. Almost all the measures used in the civic equality index are from surveys, and other indicators of organizational activity do not appear to distinguish activities or organizations in terms of racial or ethnic backgrounds. Owing to the size and distribution of minority populations in the United States, appropriate survey evidence is likely not feasible and not available across the fifty states. This inadequacy of surveys across states with respect to racial/ethnic group populations constrains a full examination of racial civic equality. However, census data for voter registration and turnout do provide adequate evidence to consider civic equality and race. And voting data appear to be the most appropriate for considering civic equality because "the voting population is the closest match in racial and ethnic terms to the population as a whole" (Verba et al. 1995, p. 237 and ch. 8). Therefore, if social capital is indeed linked to "civic equality," as social capital arguments maintain (Putnam 2000, ch. 22), then it should be most apparent regarding voting activities. Indicators of registration and turnout among the eligible population for 1992, 1994, and 1996 – which are available for most of the states and are disaggregated by racial groups – is used to examine racial civic equality.

Another dimension addressed in social capital arguments is economic inequality. The gini index of economic inequality, like the civic equality measure, does not differentiate by racial groups within states. However, census data on per capita income and poverty levels (by racial/ethnic groups and within the states) are available, and such data are used to examine racial economic equality. Analyses of civic equality and of economic equality ratios – of blacks to whites – will be discussed next and summarized in figure and table form.

The scatterplots of Figure 4-3 and Figure 4-4 summarize the registration and turnout ratios. As indicated, on the whole the evidence provides no support for the social capital thesis in that the ratios indicate negative or at best no relationships with social

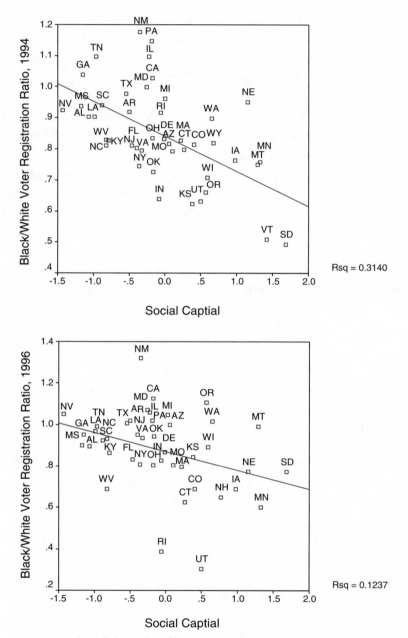

FIGURE 4-3. Social Capital and Voter Registration Ratios, 1994 and 1996

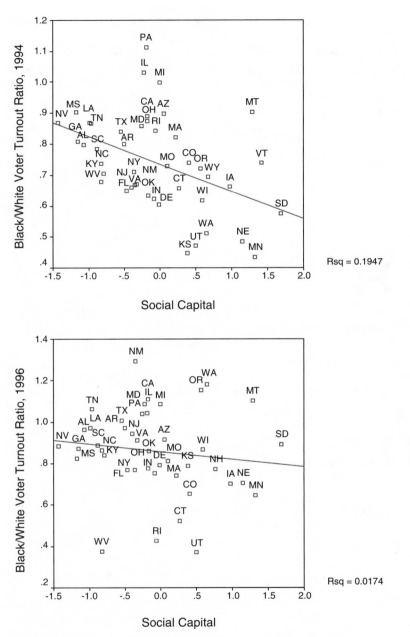

FIGURE 4-4. Social Capital and Voter Turnout Ratios, 1994 and 1996

TABLE 4-2. *Social Capital and Racial Civic Equality: Registration Ratios (within states)*

Independent Variable	Model 1	Model 2	Model 3	Model 4
Dependent variable: black/white voter registration ratio, 1992				
Social capital	−.121**	−.1246**	−.082	−.0689
	(.0487)	(.0524)	(.0522)	(.0597)
Minority diversity		−.0415		.0958
		(.1921)		(.2008)
Black poverty rates			.0059*	.0066*
			(.0034)	(.0038)
Constant	.8623****	.8771****	.6973****	.6435****
	(.0296)	(.0746)	(.0999)	(.1518)
Adj. R^2	.16	.129	.219	.195
N	28	28	28	28
Dependent variable: black/white voter registration ratio, 1994				
Social capital	−.1125****	−.0765**	−.1142****	−.0686**
	(.0257)	(.0293)	(.0267)	(.0324)
Minority diversity		.2977**		.3281**
		(.1325)		(.1432)
Black poverty rates			−.0007	.0017
			(.0029)	(.0027)
Constant	.8406****	.7421****	.861****	.6805****
	(.0193)	(.0476)	(.0876)	(.1147)
Adj. R^2	.298	.359	.282	.349
N	44	44	44	44
Dependent variable: black/white voter registration ratio, 1996				
Social capital	−.0903**	−.0228	−.093**	−.0122
	(.0376)	(.04)	(.0392)	(.0428)
Minority diversity		.5672***		.6038***
		(.1731)		(.1822)
Black poverty rates			−.001	.0025
			(.0039)	(.0036)
Constant	.8711****	.6836****	.9018****	.5988****
	(.0275)	(.0623)	(.117)	(.139)
Adj. R^2	.102	.275	.082	.265
N	43	43	43	43

Note: See notes to Table 4-1.

capital; there are no positive relationships that are also statistically significant. These findings are discussed in turn.

Examining Civic and Economic Equality Ratios Within States

Civic Equality

REGISTRATION RATIOS. Is social capital (significantly) related to better (i.e., more equal) black/white voter registration ratios in the states? The evidence emphatically indicates it is not; in fact, quite the contrary. The bivariate relationships between social capital and black/white registration ratios for 1992, 1994, and 1996 are all negative and are statistically significant, as illustrated in Figure 4-3 and affirmed in Table 4-2 (see model 1 for each year). Higher aggregate (overall) social capital is associated with larger gaps between black and white registration. Moreover, essentially the same patterns are found when a "civic culture" measure (developed by Rice and Sumberg 1997), a similar indicator of community or social capital, is examined with registration ratios. The relationships for the three years are all negative and statistically significant (at $p = .05$ or stronger).

There is also no support for the claim that social capital is positively (and significantly) related to better ratios after controlling for other factors: minority diversity, black poverty rates, or both (see models 2, 3, and 4). Indeed, for two of the three years the relationships continue to be negative and significant even after accounting for these other factors, alone or in combination. And the same is true when civic culture, another independent variable indicative of community, is examined.

TURNOUT RATIOS. As with the registration data, the evidence indicates social capital is not related to more equal black/white turnout ratios in the states. The bivariate relationship (Table 4-3, model 1 for each year) between social capital and black/white turnout for 1992, 1994, and 1996 are all negative, and for two of the three years those negative relationships are statistically significant. Again, similar relationships are found when the civic culture measure (Rice and Sumberg 1997) is examined with turnout

TABLE 4-3. *Social Capital and Racial Civic Equality: Turnout Ratios (within states)*

Independent Variable	Model 1	Model 2	Model 3	Model 4
Dependent variable: black/white voter turnout ratio, 1992				
Social capital	−.1497***	−.1487***	−.1349**	−.1255**
	(.7862)	(.0486)	(.0506)	(.058)
Minority diversity		.0121		.0692
		(.178)		(.1951)
Black poverty rates			.0022	.0027
			(.0033)	(.0037)
Constant	.7862****	.7819****	.7237****	.6848****
	(.0274)	(.0691)	(.097)	(.1475)
Adj. R^2	.120	.123	.255	.228
N	28	28	28	28
Dependent variable: black/white voter turnout ratio, 1994				
Social capital	−.0892***	−.0735**	−.0902***	−.0708*
	(.028)	(.0336)	(.0293)	(.0373)
Minority diversity		.1295		.14
		(.1519)		(.1647)
Black poverty rates			−.0004	.0006
			(.0032)	(.0034)
Constant	.7362****	.6933****	.749****	.672****
	(.021)	(.0545)	(.0956)	(.132)
Adj. R^2	.176	.17	.156	.15
N	44	44	44	44
Dependent variable: black/white voter turnout ratio, 1996				
Social capital	−.0368	.0384	−.0403	.0493
	(.0432)	(.0459)	(.0451)	(.0496)
Minority diversity		.6319***		.6691***
		(.2007)		(.2116)
Black poverty rates			−.0014	.0025
			(.0045)	(.0042)
Constant	.8575****	.6485****	.8981****	.5623****
	(.0316)	(.0723)	(.1346)	(.1614)
Adj. R^2	−.007	.173	−.029	.159
N	43	43	43	43

Note: See notes to Table 4-1.

ratios. None are positive; rather, all three are negative and one of the three is significantly so. These relationships between social capital and turnout ratios are further affirmed when controls for minority diversity, black poverty rates, or both are introduced (see Table 4-3, models 2, 3, and 4, for each year), and this same pattern holds if "civic culture" is substituted for "social capital."

In sum, there is no evidence of positive and statistically significant relationships between civic equality (i.e., black/white registration or turnout ratios) and either one of two "community" indicators (Putnam's social capital and Rice and Sumberg's civic culture), whether these factors are examined alone or while accounting for other variables. Instead, the relationships are almost always negative (for both indicators, over three years in the 1990s) and are often significant. Thus, suggestions that social capital is associated with higher civic equality regarding racial groups are *not* supported; if anything, the social capital claim is clearly contradicted. And based on other major studies of civic participation (e.g., Verba et al. 1995), we should expect to find less racial equality in other civic activities as well.

Economic Equality

POVERTY RATIOS. Is social capital positively and significantly related to better black/white poverty ratios? No; the relationship is negative (and weakly statistically significant at $p = .10, n = 48$) in the bivariate case. The bivariate relationship is also negative for the civic culture indicator but is not significant (Rice and Sumberg 1997). When the relation of social capital to black versus white poverty ratios is considered with a control for minority diversity introduced, the relationship remains negative but is no longer statistically significant (data not shown).

PER CAPITA INCOME RATIOS. Is social capital related to black/white per capita income ratios? Here the answer is a clear yes. The relationships is positive and is strongly significant (at $p = .001$), and the relationship with Rice and Sumberg's (1997) civic culture indicator is similarly significant and positive. This

is the first piece of evidence regarding economic or civic equality that is consistent with the social capital thesis. Moreover,
the strong and positive relationship between social capital (and
civic culture) and income ratios is maintained after controlling
for minority diversity. Minority diversity itself has a negative and
weakly significant relationship ($p = .10$) to per capita income
ratios.

It is interesting, then, the data indicate better per capita *income*
ratios – but no better black/white *poverty* ratios – associated
with higher social capital. What is less clear is whether more
equal income leads to more social capital, or if the reverse holds.
Social capital analyses have been ambiguous about the direction
of causality, saying only that the patterns "go together" (Putnam
2000 cf. Tarrow 1996). These data also suggest that the relationship between social class (poverty and income) and social capital
or civic culture may be more complicated and may vary more (as
a function of the specific indicators used) than previous studies
have acknowledged or explored.

The evidence on civic equality that is based on black/white
registration and turnout ratios provides no support for the claim
that higher social capital is associated with greater civic equality.
These ratio indicators are the most appropriate for examining
relative equality (i.e., within states). The evidence is consistent
and, on the whole, striking in its challenge to the social capital
thesis. It should be remembered that these ratios are derived
from the rates for minorities divided by the rates for whites;
thus, extreme (very high and/or very low) rates for either group
will affect the overall ratios. For this and other reasons, some
might argue that a more appropriate assessment of the social
capital thesis is to examine group patterns *across* states, rather
than comparing groups relative to each other *within* states.

Yet, as argued previously regarding social outcomes, within-
state comparisons are the appropriate ones for examining
racial/ethnic aspects and equality because it is within states –
and not across states – that the very notion of community is presumed to apply. Moreover, state governments exercise the major

police power and domestic policy responsibilities in the American federal system, and social capital analyses base their own evidence and arguments on within-state patterns (Putnam 2000, chs. 16–22; Rice and Sumberg 1997). Nonetheless, we examine across-state group comparisons in the next section.

Examining Rates Across States

Civic Equality: Rates

REGISTRATION RATES. Is social capital positively (and significantly) related to black registration rates – that is, rates across states? The answer is No. In the bivariate case, two of the relationships are negative and one of those negative relationships (for 1994) is significant. These findings are essentially repeated when the civic culture measure (Rice and Sumberg 1997) is substituted for the social capital one. See Table 4-4.

Social capital *is* clearly related to white voter registration rates; the bivariate relationships for all three years are strongly positive and significant, and similar (though somewhat weaker) relationships are also evident when the civic culture measure is tested.

Multivariate analysis of black registration rates with social capital, including controls for the size of a state's black population and black poverty rates, generally affirm the negative or nonrelationships found for the bivariate analysis; and this is also the case with the civic culture indicator. Analysis of white registration rates with social capital suggest that the relationships continue to be strongly and positively related to registration rates in the multivariate case.

TURNOUT RATES. Social capital bears no positive relation to better black turnout rates (Table 4.5). The bivariate relationship in 1992 is actually negative (and weakly significant, $p = .10$). For 1994 and 1996 the bivariate relationships are weakly positive, but they are not statistically significant. Similar relationships are found with the civic culture indicator of community. On the other hand, social capital *is* related to white voter turnout

TABLE 4-4. *Social Capital and Black Registration Rates (across states)*

Independent Variable	Model 1	Model 2	Model 3	Model 4
Dependent variable: black voter registration rate, 1992				
Social capital	−5.484	−.1499	−.1651	4.339
	(3.883)	(6.503)	(3.649)	(5.668)
Percentage black		.3836		.3299
population		(.3753)		(.318)
Black poverty rates			.8041***	.7914***
			(.2395)	(.2395)
Constant	62.629****	58.752****	40.131****	37.151****
	(2.354)	(4.464)	(6.993)	(7.55)
Adj. R^2	.036	.037	.309	.311
N	28	28	28	28
Dependent variable: black voter registration rate, 1994				
Social capital	−3.318*	.0417	−2.47	.3171
	(1.874)	(2.576)	(1.896)	(2.547)
Percentage black		.3874*		.3364
population		(.21)		(.2099)
Black poverty rates			.354*	.3001
			(.2048)	(.2037)
Constant	55.75****	51.799****	45.328****	43.484****
	(1.41)	(2.543)	(6.184)	(6.177)
Adj. R^2	.047	.099	.09	.124
N	44	44	44	44
Dependent variable: black voter registration rate, 1996				
Social capital	−3.329	.5367	−2.711	.6792
	(2.522)	(3.4598)	(2.608)	(3.49)
Percentage black		.4382		.4037
population		(.274)		(.2805)
Black poverty rates			.2438	.1764
			(.2583)	(.2592)
Constant	60.56****	56.114****	53.426****	51.303****
	(1.845)	(3.318)	(7.78)	(7.818)
Adj. R^2	.017	.053	.015	.041
N	43	43	43	43

Note: See notes to Table 4-1.

TABLE 4-5. *Social Capital and Black Turnout Rates (across states)*

Independent Variable	Model 1	Model 2	Model 3	Model 4
Dependent variable: black voter turnout rate, 1992)				
Social capital	−5.158*	−.3421	−2.77	1.634
	(3.026)	(5.032)	(3.244)	(5.015)
Percentage black population		.3463		.3227
		(.2904)		(.2814)
Black poverty rates			.3609	.3485
			(.213)	(.2119)
Constant	52.047****	48.547****	41.95****	39.035****
	(1.835)	(3.454)	(6.217)	(6.68)
Adj. R^2	.066	.081	.129	.14
N	28	28	28	28
Dependent variable: black voter turnout rate, 1994				
Social capital	.8462	2.391	.6467	2.286
	(1.653)	(2.34)	(1.728)	(2.365)
Percentage black population		.1782		.1978
		(.1907)		(.1949)
Black poverty rates			−.0834	−.1151
			(.1866)	(.1891)
Constant	35.695****	33.878****	38.151****	37.066****
	(1.243)	(2.31)	(5.636)	(5.734)
Adj. R^2	−.018	−.021	−.037	−.037
N	44	44	44	44
Dependent variable: black voter turnout rate, 1996				
Social capital	2.039	6.413*	2.273	6.4204*
	(2.508)	(3.409)	(2.619)	(3.458)
Percentage black population		.4957*		.4938*
		(.27)		(.2568)
Black poverty rates			.092	.0095
			(.259)	(.2568)
Constant	49.686****	44.656****	46.994****	44.396****
	(1.835)	(3.269)	(7.811)	(7.748)
Adj. R^2	−.008	.047	−.03	.023
N	43	43	43	43

Note: See notes to Table 4-1.

rates in the bivariate case, as it was with white registration rates; the relationships for each of the three years are positive and strong. And the relationships of the civic culture measure of community with white turnout rates are comparable to these. Thus, the bivariate evidence provides no support for the suggestion that *black* rates of registration or of turnout are significantly higher where there is higher aggregate social capital (or "civic culture"), only the rates for whites are higher where there is higher social capital.

Analysis of black turnout rates and social capital – including controls for the size of a state's black population and black poverty rates – generally affirm the nonrelationships found in the bivariate analysis, with one exception. The relationship between social capital and the black turnout rate for 1996 is positive and weakly significant ($p = .10$) after accounting for the size of the black population and black poverty. But this relationship does not hold when the civic culture measure of community is substituted for the social capital indicator. The relationships of social capital to white turnout remain positive and strong even when we control for other factors.

To summarize: the *ratios* of black/white registration and turnout shows that there is no evidence whatsoever to support claims of higher racial civic equality. And there is at most extremely limited evidence to support claims of black civic equality regarding rates of registration and turnout, assuming one accepts that rates are appropriate to consider in the first place. In clear contrast, the relations between white turnout rates and social capital are consistently positive and strong.

This evidence on civic equality – on registration and turnout ratios and rates for racial ethnic groups – strongly implies that the civic equality identified and touted by social capital studies is the result of higher levels for whites. These levels are imbedded within and disproportionately affect the civic equality measure (the dependent variable) as well as the social capital index (the independent variable). Thus, there is good reason to suppose that findings of "community" being strongly related to civic equality are largely if not solely due to patterns in states with large white and small minority populations, that is, in racially homogeneous contexts. In other words, what is asserted as *general* evidence of U.S. civic equality being associated with social capital (Putnam 2000, pp. 358–61; cf. Rice and Sumberg 1997) is, rather, an artifact of white social capital and civic participation and perhaps of relative racial homogeneity in a number of states. But social capital analyses conflate the differing results for minorities, confusing whites' condition with the general condition and thus incorrectly making broad claims of equality that mask what is quite possibly a situation of racial inequality. In short, the general assertions of the social capital thesis are shown to be actually partial and bounded – and certainly as they apply to issues of racial civic equality. These remarks are consistent with those of Verba et al. (1995, p. 509) concerning "voice and equality"; their analysis of "voluntary activity" [akin to "civic-ness"] in American politics suggests that the public's voice is often loud, sometimes clear, *but rarely equal"* (emphasis added). The inequality they find is based primarily on racial and income factors.

Economic Equality: Rates

POVERTY RATES. Is social capital related to black poverty rates? The evidence from the bivariate relationships suggests that it is. The relationship is negative and significant ($p = .01$); a slightly stronger relationship ($p = .001$) is found with civic culture. This indicates that black poverty rates *are* lower where there is more aggregate social capital, which is consistent with the social capital thesis. But again the direction of causation is uncertain; social capital studies have not been clear on this point (Putnam 2000). Furthermore, this positive relationship of social capital to black poverty rate does not hold when we control for the percentage of black population in a state.

An interesting result is that social capital is not related to white poverty rates; in the bivariate case there is a weakly negative but nonsignificant relationship (although there is a weakly negative, significant, $p = .10$ relationship between Rice and Sumberg's "civic culture" indicator and white poverty rates). White poverty rates might be slightly lower where there is more civic culture, but it is at most a weak relationship and again, it is unclear which is the cause and which the effect.

PER CAPITA INCOME RATES. The bivariate relationship of social capital to black per capita income rates is positive but not significant; this is also the case after controlling for percentage of black population. On the other hand, the relationship between black per capita income and the civic culture indicator of community is strongly significant ($p = .001$) and positive, and it remains so (at $p = .05$) after controlling for percentage of black population.

The relationship between white per capita income and social capital is weakly negative and not significant (it is positive but not significant for the "civic culture" measure). Neither does social capital bear a significant relation to white per capita income after controlling for black population. Yet civic culture and white per capita income are positively and significantly related after controlling for black population.

These findings on social capital in relation to poverty and per capita income rates are difficult to interpret. They may provide some support for the social capital claims regarding economic equality, but how and how much is less clear because causal direction is seldom addressed in social capital studies. The relations of social capital to black and with white rates of poverty and income do not consistently point in the same direction. Moreover, different indicators of community – that is, social capital and civic culture – produce different findings, so the precise meaning and measurement of "community" seem to matter.

The ambiguity of the present findings on economic equality, compared with the ostensible strength and clarity of *BA*'s findings (Putnam 2000, ch. 22), are thus somewhat confusing. However, it is quite probable that findings on equitable income distribution that are based on gini coefficients – which measure social class but do not directly measure racial inequality – may be due to white patterns, especially since economic equality so measured tends to be highest in more racially homogeneous states (see Putnam 2000, p. 360). In any case, it certainly seems that economic inequality, in itself and in relation to racial inequality, is substantially more complicated than social capital studies have recognized.

CONCLUSION

The systematic examination in this chapter of social outcomes, civic equality, and economic equality provides virtually no support for, and often contradicts, major claims of the social capital thesis. The evidence developed here that social outcomes for minorities are no better (and are often worse) for minorities in high–social capital settings – which directly contradicts BA's claims – has been strongly reaffirmed in subsequent research that has also provided support for the racial diversity thesis (see Hawes et al. 2006). Likewise, the patterns revealed by black/white within-state ratios on several dimensions are almost always clearly at odds with the social capital thesis, and the contradictory findings are often statistically significant. These patterns change little when rates (i.e., situations across states) are considered or when an alternative indicator (civic culture) of community is used in place of social capital.

In the aggregate, higher diversity (and lower social capital) is related to overall worse social outcomes, while lower diversity (and high social capital) is related to overall better outcomes. Higher diversity is, however, associated with relatively "less bad" outcomes for minorities, while less diversity (and high social capital) is associated with relatively worse outcomes for minorities. This suggests that if sizable minorities can mobilize to achieve representation in formal government bodies, then they can diminish (though not eliminate) unequal outcomes (Meier and Stewart 1991; Hawes et al. 2006). This also seems to imply that minorities tend to do relatively better when certain issues are addressed in governmental arenas than when left to the informal, civic realm (Schattschneider 1960). Should that be the case, it adds another layer of doubt concerning the implications of social capital for matters of racial equality: higher social capital may diminish economic inequality among whites, but its impacts are negligible (or nonexistent) when the racial dimension of inegalitarian traditions is also considered.

The data presented in this chapter indicate that Putnam's (2000) provocative findings – that high aggregate social capital has powerful beneficial effects – are, in fact, dubious and limited at best. Because those findings of beneficial effects are the pillars of evidence on its behalf, the social capital thesis appears still more profoundly problematic. The data presented here demonstrate that those alleged salutary effects are attributable and confined to the white (nonminority) condition, not the minority condition. Hence the findings heralded in major social capital studies are in reality circumscribed by racial context; that is, they are racially contingent. The evidence implies that there remains a systemic, two-tiered quality of white versus black social conditions – certainly not the salutary and equal conditions found by social capital studies.

5

Voter Turnout and Other Forms of Participation in Context

with Caroline Tolbert

Social capital studies assert that there are strong beneficial consequences of social capital on civic and economic equality as well as on social outcomes (Putnam 2000). Those assertions were analyzed in the preceding chapter using measures based on *relative* ethnic indicators, for example, minority versus white ratios. When examined in this light, the asserted impacts of social capital on social outcomes and on civic and economic equality were not supported and often were flatly contradicted. We now turn to another area in which salutary effects of social capital have been asserted – political participation and consider this in a more aggregated and (in certain respects) a more comprehensive way than in the previous chapter.

To explore the relation of racial diversity to social capital in terms of political participation, three approaches are applied. These include: an (1) analysis of the direct effects of racial diversity and of social capital on states' participation rates; (2) an account of the overlapping effects (or endogeneity) in the relationship between social capital and participation rates; and (3) a discussion of the interaction effects of race and social capital.

This chapter is co-authored with Caroline Tolbert, an Associate Professor of Political Science at the University of Iowa.

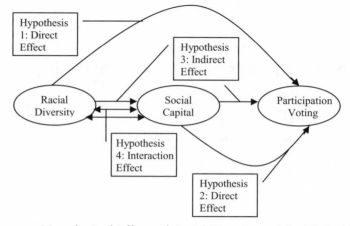

FIGURE 5-1. Hypothesized Effects of Racial Diversity and Social Capital on Participation

In order to assess the questions under review, a series of propositions are offered that juxtapose and then bring together the racial diversity and social capital theses. These propositions are summarized in Figure 5-1 and are discussed next.

FOUR THESES

Direct Racial Effects Thesis

A racial diversity interpretation suggests that states with higher racial diversity will have lower voter turnout rates in elections, both midterm and presidential, over the period of study. Previous research (cf. Hill and Leighley 1999; Key 1949; Hero 1998) leads us to expect depressed turnout rates among whites and racial minorities in southern and nonsouthern states with higher racial diversity (i.e., African American, Latino, or Asian populations), particularly in the most bifurcated settings (see Chapter 3). Although some research indicates that turnout is relatively high in heterogeneous settings, evidence focused on racial diversity – high bifurcation per se – indicates lower aggregate turnout. The first hypothesis examined, then, is that exclusion (or inclusion) and inequality associated with varying degrees of state racial diversity can independently encourage or inhibit political participation, regardless of a community's level of social capital.

Direct Social Capital Effects Thesis

As hypothesized and found in previous research (Putnam 2000), states with higher levels of social capital will have higher voter turnout rates in elections (both midterm and presidential). Stronger civic engagement, as indicated by levels of social capital, is expected to be directly associated with increased political participation regardless of state demographic composition.

Indirect Effects Thesis

As we have argued, social capital's direct effect on political behavior may be less than indicated by the literature (Putnam 2000) in that its alleged salutary effects on turnout rates may be conditioned by racial diversity. States with higher racial diversity are expected to have lower levels of social capital; social boundaries between different racial and ethnic groups are expected to lessen interactions and the development of community bonds, leading in turn to lower overall political participation. For example, more homogeneous states (with low racial diversity) are expected to have higher levels of social capital and higher electoral participation rates.

Interactive Effects Thesis

Another possibility, which has been implied but not directly examined previously, is that racial diversity and social capital *interact* in their impact on voter turnout rates. Beneficial effects of social capital on turnout rates may well be reduced in states with high racial diversity. Whereas previous discussion has indicated that racial diversity shapes, and perhaps even precedes levels of social capital in the states, this analysis suggests that the effects of race and community are interactive and simultaneous (cf. Orren and Skowronek 2004).

These hypothesized sets of relationships are examined over a 22-year period (1980–2002) using pooled fifty-state data to assess the direct, indirect, and conditional effects of state racial diversity and social capital on voter turnout).[1] To examine the first two theses, we examine separately the impact of state racial diversity and social capital on voter turnout rates while controlling for other state-level factors known to affect participation rates. For the third hypothesis, analysis is undertaken with state racial diversity (and other variables) used to predict overall levels of social capital in the states and, in turn, the probability of social capital predicting voter turnout rates. Finally, to test the fourth proposition, interaction terms are used to consider the (potential) simultaneous effects of racial diversity and social capital on voter turnout rates in the states.

ANALYTICAL APPROACH

The variable to be explained (the dependent variable) is average state voter eligible population (VEP) turnout, a measure of voting not previously used in research on the effects of racial diversity or social capital. Traditionally, turnout has been calculated as simply a ratio: the number who voted divided by the size of the voting-age population (VAP). But this divisor includes people who are ineligible to vote, most notably noncitizens, immigrants, and felons – groups that have grown considerably since 1972.

---

[1] The data are analyzed using cross-sectional time series analysis with panel corrected standard errors (PCSE), statistically controlling for variation between states and over time. Beck and Katz (1995) make a strong case for using PCSE over random effects models for pooled data when the number of time periods is relatively small compared to the number of panels ($T < N$). Our models of presidential and midterm election turnout have 6 time periods (T) and 50 panels (N), with each state as a panel. The use of PCSE corrects for serial correlation in calculating the standard errors of the regression coefficients. Since these data are panel dominated with a small number of time periods, some scholars have suggested that the use of PCSE may introduce bias. The models also include year dummy variables to further control for heteroskedasticity and autocorrelation, which may bias the standard errors of the regression coefficients.

When excluding these groups of ineligible voters, it has been found that VEP turnout for the last eight elections has averaged about 56 percent, with no real downward trend (McDonald and Popkin 2001).

Since a high proportion of noncitizens and felons reside in the western and southern states, which include the states (i.e., California and Florida) with the highest racial diversity, this might affect the results of previous research by misestimating the impact of racial diversity on voter turnout (Hill and Leighley 1999). Estimates of VEP turnout have been created by removing ineligible voters from the population estimates (McDonald and Popkin 2001). Those estimates – measures of the votes cast for president or in congressional races in midterm years, divided by each state's VEP (McDonald and Popkin 2001) – are used here as the dependent variable. Statewide VEP turnout data are available only since 1980, and the impact of race and social capital on voter turnout is examined here in elections from 1980 through 2002. These years parallel those included in the social capital index (of 1975–1995), and the data for diversity and are thus appropriate. As with other indicators of turnout (see Rosenstone and Hansen 1993; Jackson, Brown, and Wright 1998), there is considerable variation in VEP turnout across the fifty states, with generally lower turnout in the South.

Substantial previous scholarship (Key 1949; Hill and Leighley 1999; Hero 1998; Meier and Stewart 1991) has found that race plays an important role in subnational U.S. politics. This racial effect is found nationwide (i.e., even outside of the traditional South) and in both the pre– and post–civil rights era (Hill and Leighley 1999; cf. Putnam 2000). Here, state ethnic diversity is measured with indices based on 1980, 1990, and 2000 U.S. Census data on the percentage of Anglo, Latino, African American, and Asian populations (this procedure is similar to that used in some previous studies – e.g., Hero and Tolbert 1996; Hero 1998, p. 12). We also look at whether there are any nonlinear effects of racial diversity on turnout rates (which is also explored by including a "squared term"). Because social capital

has previously been found to be a leading explanation of participation rates in the American states (Putnam 2000), the expectation is that states with higher social capital will have high voter
turnout rates. As in other sections of this book, fifty-state data
for the overall social capital index were drawn from Putnam
(2000). To check for any nonlinear effects of social capital on
participation rates, a squared measure of the social capital index,
is included. Since racial diversity and social capital are highly
correlated, these two variables are initially tested separately
(see Table 5-1).

Other demographic, institutional, and economic factors influence turnout rates across the fifty states and should therefore be
accounted for in the analysis. We control for southern states,
which have traditionally experienced much lower turnout rates
as a legacy of Jim Crow laws and one-party dominance. We also
take into account the presence of other statewide elections –
gubernatorial and U.S. Senate races – that may boost turnout (a
dummy variable is used in both cases, coded 1 if the state had
such a race and zero otherwise). Previous research has shown
that voter registration requirements have a noticeable effect on
statewide turnout: more stringent registration laws lead to lower
voter turnout (Wolfinger and Rosenstone 1980). Registration
requirements are measured by how many days before an election one must register to vote; for example, states with Election Day registration or no required voter registration are coded
zero, and states that require registration a month before the
election are coded 30. Recent research finds that ballot measures boost turnout rates in the American states (M. Smith
2001; Tolbert, Grummel, and Smith 2001); to control for this
potential effect of "direct democracy," the number of initiatives
appearing on state ballots for each year in the times series is
included.

Voter turnout rates differ by socioeconomic status: those with
higher income, education, and occupational status are considerably more likely to vote (Campbell et al. 1960; Wolfinger and
Rosenstone 1980; Verba et al. 1995). To acknowledge the likely

effects of education, the percentage of each state's population with a high-school degree or higher is examined. Per capita income over the 22-year period for each state is measured with data from the U.S. Census. To control for income inequality, we use "gini coefficients" that measure the disparity between the wealth of a state's top-quartile income group and its lowest-quartile income group (Langer 1999). States with wealthier and more educated populations and with more socioeconomic equality are anticipated to have high turnout rates over time, while lower aggregate (per capita) income and education levels and higher income inequality should dampen participation rates.

Previous research on voter turnout suggests that presidential and midterm elections should be analyzed separately owing to the substantially higher turnout in the former. Accordingly, we undertook separate presidential and midterm election year analyses for each of the four arguments evaluated. Thus, we considered whether there are significant variations in turnout rates over time in relation to diversity and social capital – and whether there are distinct effects in presidential versus midterm elections.

RESULTS

Assessing Direct Racial Effects

The results from analyzing the effects of state racial diversity and of social capital on voter turnout rates in presidential and midterm elections are presented in Table 5-1 and Table 5-2. A consistent result is that racial diversity and social capital each shape overall voter turnout rates over time in the southern *and* nonsouthern states, a finding that is consistent with both the direct racial diversity and the social capital effects theses.

The first two columns of Table 5-1 show that states with higher ethnic diversity have lower turnout rates over time in both midterm and presidential elections (when other factors are held constant). The effect of race on voter turnout appears to

TABLE 5-1. *Direct Effects of Racial Diversity and Social Capital on Voter Turnout, 1980–2002*

	Model			
	1	2	3	4
Dependent variable	Turnout for pres. elec.	Turnout for midterm elec.	Turnout for pres. elec.	Turnout for midterm elec.
Racial diversity index	−23.79 (5.22) $p < .00$	−19.88 (9.04) $p < .03$		
(Racial diversity)^2	12.82 (7.20) $p < .07$	14.95 (10.07) $p < .14$		
Social capital index			7.86 (.59) $p < .00$	2.59 (.67) $p < .00$
(Social capital)^2			−1.06 (.12) $p < .00$	.78 (.19) $p < .00$
South	−3.71 (.43) $p < .00$	−2.91 (.69) $p < .00$	−1.04 (.55) $p < .06$	−1.71 (.85) $p < .04$
Number of initiatives on ballot	.37 (.07) $p < .00$	.59 (.06) $p < .00$	.13 (.06) $p < .02$	.55 (.07) $p < .00$
Senate election	.43 (.59) $p < .47$	1.96 (.21) $p < .00$	.32 (.49) $p < .51$	2.18 (.15) $p < .00$
Governor election	.16 (.37) $p < .67$	2.40 (.25) $p < .00$	.06 (.38) $p < .88$	2.62 (.26) $p < .00$
% high-school graduates	.25 (.05) $p < .00$	.58 (.054) $p < .00$	.14 (.04) $p < .00$	.19 (.05) $p < .00$
Income inequality (gini coefficients)	69.37 (15.37) $p < .00$	63.57 (13.96) $p < .00$	49.20 (12.24) $p < .00$	34.02 (13.83) $p < .01$
Registration req. (closing date)	−.18 (.02) $p < .00$	−.17 (.03) $p < .00$	−.17 (.02) $p < .00$	−.12 (.02) $p < .00$
Per capita income	.0004 (.0001) $p < .000$	−.0001 (.0002) $p < .465$	.0004 (.00005) $p < .00$	−.0001 (.0002) $p < .56$
1984	1.21 (.08) $p < .00$		1.24 (.07) $p < .00$	
1986		−11.19 (.69) $p < .00$		−5.92 (.78) $p < .00$

	Model			
	1	2	3	4
1988	−6.41 (.84) $p < .00$		−4.66 (.59) $p < .00$	
1990		−9.33 (.64) $p < .00$		−5.02 (.80) $p < .00$
1992	1.34 (.82) $p < .10$		1.88 (.61) $p < .00$	
1994		−8.55 (.64) $p < .00$		−4.18 (.77) $p < .00$
1996	−7.98 (.89) $p < .00$		−7.22 (.67) $p < .00$	
1998		−11.23 (.87) $p < .00$		−7.13 (1.05) $p < .00$
2000	−8.78 (1.29) $p < .00$		−8.00 (1.00) $p < .00$	
2002		−11.54 (1.79) $p < .00$		−5.97 (1.89) $p < .00$
Constant	13.00 (8.76)	−13.10 (8.01)	15.89 (6.53)	13.14 (6.50)
Wald chi²	732190.89 $p < .00$	348000.20 $p < .00$	11966.15 $p < .00$	551820.08 $p < .00$

Notes: Cross-sectional time series data for the 50 states. Unstandardized linear regression coefficients with panel corrected standard errors in parentheses; probabilities based on a two-tailed test. The number of observations for each of the 50 panels is 6 for presidential elections and 6 for midterm elections; $N = 299$ for model 1, 296 for model 2, 287 for model 3, and 284 for model 4. Findings are unchanged when models are reestimated with an autorecursive option to correct for heteroskedasticity.

be direct and linear (the squared term for state racial diversity is not statistically significant in midterm elections and does not satisfy traditional confidence intervals for statistical significance in presidential elections). As state racial diversity increases, voter turnout rates are lower, and there is no leveling-off effect after reaching a certain threshold (and only a slight drop-off in presidential elections). The effect of racial diversity is more pronounced in presidential elections, but the impact of this variable

TABLE 5-2. *Predicted Effect: Change in Voter Turnout by State Racial Diversity and Social Capital*

Racial Diversity	VEP Turnout, Presidential Elections	Level of Social Capital	VEP Turnout, Presidential Elections
Very low (−2SD)	64.28%	Very low (−2SD)	37.39%
Low (−1SD)	60.32%	Low (−1SD)	43.45%
Average (mean)	56.23%	Average (mean)	49.51%
High (+1SD)	52.23%	High (+1SD)	55.56%
Very high (+2SD)	48.19%	Very high (+2SD)	61.61%
High minus low	−8%	High minus low	+12%

Note: Predicted values (probabilities) estimated with a do file in STATA. To simulate different levels of state racial diversity and social capital, the variable was checked at its mean and then at one and two standard deviations (SD) above and below its mean. The simulations assume a senate and governor election on the ballot; all other explanatory variables were held constant at their means. Predicted values calculated from the coefficients reported columns 1 and 3 of Table 5-1.

is comparable in both election contexts (−.24 presidential and −.20 midterm). More diversity consistently results in lower participation rates, regardless of the type of election.

This pattern is even more apparent when we examine predicted probabilities of voter turnout at different levels of diversity based on the model reported in column 1 of Table 5-1. All other state demographic, political, and economic predictors of voter turnout are held constant (at their mean or modal values) for the simulations. As indicated in Table 5-2, states with the lowest levels of diversity (2 standard deviations below the mean level of diversity, the most "homogeneous") have turnouts of 64 percent. In contrast, the most diverse states – those at the highest levels (2 standard deviations above the mean) of minority diversity – have a turnout of about 48 percent. *Ceteris paribus,* states with high racial diversity (defined as 1 standard deviation above the mean) have on average 8 percent lower voter turnout in presidential elections than states with low racial diversity (1 standard deviation below the mean); see Table 5-2. States with the highest racial diversity are predicted to have turnouts of 8 percent less than the average state in terms of diversity in presidential elections, other things being equal. The independent and direct effect of race on voter turnout rates is indeed substantial.

This finding supports previous research (Hill and Leighley 1999) based on an analysis of 1950–1992 (rather than 1980–2002) data, a different measure of racial diversity, and a different measure of voter turnout (VAP rather than VEP turnout rates). Hence our results affirm that the effect of race on vote turnout in the American states is consistent regardless of how the specific analysis is structured, how the critical predictor variable (racial diversity) is measured, or the time period. Despite the forty or so years since the height of the civil rights era, the effects of race in dampening participation rates continues to be apparent in the latter decades of the twentieth and into the early twenty-first century. Although Hill and Leighley argue that mobilizing institutions – specifically, political parties – mediate the relationship between racial diversity and turnout rates, here we find that varying degrees of state racial homogeneity or diversity independently encourage or inhibit political participation apart from mediating institutions.

Assessing Direct Social Capital Effects

Social capital has a strong and positive impact on voter turnout rates over time, as previous research has also shown (Putnam 2000; Putnam 1993; Elazar 1984). Columns 3 and 4 of Table 5-1 show that states with high levels of overall social capital have higher turnout rates over the 22-year period in both midterm and presidential elections when we control for other factors. Unlike racial diversity, however, social capital appears to have a *non*linear effect on voter participation rates (since the squared term is statistically significant in both models); this means that the positive effects of social capital on participation rates level off after a certain point. Whereas the effect of racial diversity on voter turnout was essentially similar across types of election, the effect of social capital on turnout rates is more than double in presidential than in midterm elections.

Exploring this issue further with simulations, we can see in Table 5-2 that states with high social capital (at least 1 standard deviation above the mean) are predicted to have on average 12 percent higher voter turnout in presidential elections than states with low social capital (1 standard deviation below the mean), *ceteris paribus*: high–social capital states are predicted to have 56 percent turnout, on average, while low social capital states have on average 44 percent turnout in presidential elections. States with the very highest levels of social capital have about 12 percent higher turnout than those with average levels of social capital. These findings corroborate yet also expand on findings about the effects of aggregate social capital on political participation (Putnam 2000).

The direct effects of racial diversity and of social capital on political participation in presidential elections are of similar magnitude but in opposite directions, -8 percent and $+12$ percent, respectively (see Table 5-2). These are nontrivial differences that may be enough to affect close elections. Clearly racial diversity and social capital matter for overall turnout. The impact of many of the other variables from the analysis (Table 5-1) is also in accord with previous research.

For example, southern states consistently have lower turnout rates and states with more initiatives on the ballot have high participation in both midterm and presidential election, as also shown other research (Tolbert et al. 2001; Tolbert and Smith 2005). A senator or governor's race on the ballot increases turnout in midterm elections, while a more educated state population consistently is associated with a boost in participation rates regardless of election-year context. Wealthier states (as measured by per capita income) have higher turnout, but only in presidential election years; also consistent with previous research is our finding that more stringent registration requirements (earlier closing dates) results in lower voter turnout

(Wolfinger and Rosenstone 1980). An anomalous finding – one that is not consistent with previous research – is that higher income *in*equality is associated with increased turnout rates, holding other factors constant. This finding suggests that once racial diversity, geographic factors, state income, and education levels are taken into account, the independent effect of economic inequality may not actually lessen political participation.

Assessing Indirect Effects

Diversity and social capital may also work in some combination to shape political participation in the states, and thus their effects may be indirect. One way to think about the relations between race, social capital, and voter turnout is in terms of exogenous and endogenous explanations of political behavior. If one assumes that the demographic composition of a state's population is more likely to precede or in some way "cause" the density, quality, and general nature of social networks and formation of community (i.e., the levels of social capital) than vice versa, then state racial diversity may be understood as the exogenous factor and social capital as the endogenous explanation. Although perhaps debatable or at least more complex than suggested here, this claim is consistent with concepts and arguments regarding "color lines" (DuBois 1935), "racial formation" (Omi and Winant 1986) and "racial orders" (King and Smith 2005) in American politics. That is, social relations and sense of community are seen as emerging – to a substantial degree – from groups' racial and demographic traits.

We also undertook an assessment of multiple causes of political participation that emphasized (of course) state racial diversity and social capital. If state racial diversity influences social capital, state demographic populations would be expected to be a (statistically) significant predictor of levels of social capital. In the first stage, a state racial diversity measure is created using 1980 and 1990 U.S. Census demographic data (to preserve time order) as well as a set of control variables (measured using 1980 and 1990 data) used to predict levels of overall state social capital. In the second stage, voter turnout is calculated as a function of the predicted values of social capital and a set of control variables.

As anticipated and consistent with earlier evidence, racial diversity is indeed a significant predictor of social capital in the first stage (see Table 5-3, column 1), even when we control for other socioeconomic factors. Racial environments shape levels of community or social capital; states with more homogeneous white populations, for instance, tend to have higher social capital even after socioeconomic factors are taken into account. And the predicted value of social capital is positively related to greater voter turnout in both presidential (Table 5-3, column 2) and midterm (column 3) elections. Although social capital does lead to increased political participation, these data indicate that the relationship between social capital and participation is partially endogenous; in other words, it is driven by the state's level of racial diversity. Homogenous white contexts are associated with higher social capital and, in turn, increased political participation. Others have found that political institutions mediate the relationship between race and voter turnout (Hill and Leighley 1999); the evidence presented here suggests that social capital may likewise mediate the relationship between race and political engagement.

Until now we have been discussing evidence for a direct effect and an indirect effect of racial diversity or social capital on political participation rates, where in the latter case social capital mediates the relationship between racial diversity and voter turnout. But it is surely possible that race and social capital may interact simultaneously to influence turnout rates in the states. That is, the two social factors are so interconnected that they cannot be entirely disentangled, making it difficult to decide which precedes which and thus suggesting that an analysis of interactive effects would be useful.

TABLE 5-3. *Indirect Effects of Race on Voter Turnout, 1980–2002*

	Model/Stage		
	1	2	3
Dependent variable	Overall levels of social cap., 1990	Turnout for pres. elec., 1992–2000	Turnout for midterm elec., 1990–2002
Racial diversity, 1980 and 1990	−2.10 (.14) $p < .00$		
Probability of social capital		6.79 (.89) $p < .00$	4.24 (1.01) $p < .00$
South		−4.03 (.40) $p < .00$	−3.35 (.57) $p < .00$
Number of initiatives on ballot		.35 (.07) $p < .00$	.61 (.06) $p < .00$
Senate election		.38 (.61) $p < .54$	1.94 (.20) $p < .00$
Governor election		.22 (.37) $p < .55$	2.47 (.28) $p < .00$
% high-school graduates	.04 (.01) $p < .00$	−.01 (.06) $p < .84$	.41 (.06) $p < .00$
Income inequality (gini coefficients)	−7.03 (1.16) $p < .00$	112.67 (19.27) $p < .00$	88.97 (16.74) $p < .00$
Registration req. (closing date)		−.19 (.02) $p < .00$	−.18 (.03) $p < .00$
Per capita income	−.00002 (.68e-07) $p < .01$	.001 (.0001) $p < .00$	−.0001 (.0002) $p < .65$
1984		1.24 (.08) $p < .00$	
1986			−10.94 (.62) $p < .00$
1988		−6.30 (.80) $p < .00$	
1990			−9.14 (.61) $p < .00$
1992		1.41 (.80) $p < .08$	

(*continued*)

TABLE 5-3 *(continued)*

	Model/Stage		
	1	2	3
1994			−8.36 (.63)
			p < .00
1996		−7.87 (.86)	
		p < .00	
1998			−10.96 (.82)
			p < .00
2000		−8.50 (1.25)	
		p < .00	
2002			−11.01 (1.67)
			p < .00
Constant	.74 (.72)	7.13 (8.93)	−15.58 (7.79)
Wald chi²	2237.64	317739.56	936849.40
	p < .00	p < .00	p < .00
N	576	299	296

Notes: Cross-sectional time series data for the 50 states. Unstandardized linear regression coefficients with panel corrected standard errors in parentheses; probabilities based on a two-tailed test. The number of observations for each of the 50 panels is 6 for presidential elections and 6 for midterm elections. For model 1, the explanatory variable was measured only in 1980 decade and year 1990 to preserve time order, since the social captial index is calculated from data through 1990.

Assessing Interactive Effects

In this section we examine the possibility of an interactive effect of racial diversity and social capital on voter turnout rates. Two different interactions were constructed. We started by creating, a dummy variable for states with high racial diversity, where states with diversity above the mean were coded 1 and those below the mean were coded 0; Multiplying this variable by the social capital index creates the interaction term; the results are presented in Table 5-4 for presidential elections (column 1) and midterm elections (column 2). As shown in the table, there is evidence of a conditional relationship between race and social capital, supporting the hypothesis; however, the

TABLE 5-4. *Conditional Effects of Race and Social Capital on Voter Turnout,*
1980–2002

	Model			
	1	2	3	4
Dependent variable	Turnout for pres. elec.	Turnout for midterm elec.	Turnout for pres. elec.	Turnout for midterm elec.
Social capital × high racial diversity states (coded 1 above the mean)	1.47 (.53) *p* < .01	−1.61 (.79) *p* < .04		
High racial diversity states (coded 1 above the mean)	−3.87 (.81) *p* < .00	1.64 (1.29) *p* < .20		
Social capital × racial diversity (index)			−.21 (1.93) *p* < .91	−4.17 (1.78) *p* < .02
Racial diversity index			−7.61 (3.14) *p* < .02	2.09 (1.80) *p* < .25
Social capital index	3.14 (.20) *p* < .00	2.69 (.42) *p* < .00	3.35 (.35) *p* < .00	5.72 (.32) *p* < .00
South	−1.09 (.42) *p* < .01	−1.50 (.91) *p* < .10	−2.20 (.50) *p* < .00	−1.66 (.78) *p* < .03
Number of initiatives on ballot	.17 (.06) *p* < .00	.58 (.09) *p* < .00	.21 (.06) *p* < .00	.59 (.08) *p* < .00
Senate election	.31 (.53) *p* < .56	2.12 (.12) *p* < .00	.31 (.49) *p* < .53	2.13 (.14) *p* < .00
Governor election	−.18 (.34) *p* < .60	2.48 (.32) *p* < .00	−.23 (.38) *p* < .54	2.58 (.28) *p* < .00
% high-school graduates	.17 (.04) *p* < .00	.18 (.06) *p* < .00	.15 (.04) *p* < .00	.18 (.05) *p* < .00
Income inequality (gini coefficients)	54.81 (12.49) *p* < .00	36.81 (15.21) *p* < .02	62.50 (13.24) *p* < .00	40.18 (14.92) *p* < .01
Registration req. (closing date)	−.16 (.02) *p* < .00	−.11 (.02) *p* < .00	−.14 (.02) *p* < .00	−.11 (.03) *p* < .00

(continued)

TABLE 5-4 *(continued)*

	Model			
	1	2	3	4
Per capita income	.0005 (.00005)	−.0001 (.0002)	.0005 (.00005)	−.0001 (.0002)
	$p < .00$	$p < .656$	$p < .00$	$p < .66$
1984	1.12 (.07)		1.11 (.07)	
	$p < .00$		$p < .00$	
1986		−5.85 (.88)		−5.93 (.84)
		$p < .00$		$p < .00$
1988	−5.38 (.65)		−5.32 (.67)	
	$p < .00$		$p < .00$	
1990		−4.90 (.92)		−4.70 (.81)
		$p < .00$		$p < .00$
1992	1.22 (.65)		1.85 (.66)	
	$p < .06$		$p < .01$	
1994		−4.01 (.93)		−3.83 (.78)
		$p < .00$		$p < .00$
1996	−8.05 (.72)		−7.45 (.71)	
	$p < .00$		$p < .00$	
1998		−4.03 (1.21)		−6.81 (1.07)
		$p < .00$		$p < .00$
2000	−9.27 (1.05)		−8.52 (1.03)	
	$p < .00$		$p < .00$	
2002		−5.79 (2.13)		−5.55 (1.96)
		$p < .01$		$p < .01$
Constant	15.10 (6.98)	9.77 (7.71)	13.34 (7.18)	8.61 (8.12)
Wald chi^2	119280.43	146000.18	247043.81	47212.58
	$p < .00$	$p < .00$	$p < .00$	$p < .00$

Notes: Cross-sectional time series data for the 50 states. Unstandardized linear regression coefficients with panel corrected standard errors in parentheses; probabilities based on a two-tailed test. The number of observations for each of the 50 panels is 6 for presidential elections and 6 for midterm elections; $N = 287$ for models 1 and 3, 284 for models 2 and 4.

effect is most pronounced in midterm elections. Both interaction terms are statistically significant, which indicates that the positive effects of social capital on voter turnout vary by levels of racial diversity. This also means that the positive effects of social capital or community in states with high racial diversity are diminished.[2]

We undertook probability simulations in order to further probe this conditional relationship. The simulations are calculated only for *high – racial diversity states* (those with above-average racial diversity), holding all other state demographic, economic, and political factors constant but assuming a senate or governor's race is on the election ballot. The results, presented in Table 5-5, indicate that states with high social capital (1 standard deviation above the mean) have, on average: (a) 7 percent higher voter turnout in presidential elections than states with low social capital (1 standard deviation below the mean) – 61 versus 54 percent – holding all other factors constant; and (b) 2 percent higher voter turnout in midterm elections than states with low social capital. In states with above average racial diversity, the favorable effects of social capital on voter turnout rates are reduced to 7 percent in presidential elections and to 2 percent in midterm elections, *ceteris paribus*. This compares with a 12-percent boost in turnout based on social capital alone, for example, not taking state racial diversity into account (cf. Table 5-2). These results indicate that, in states with high racial diversity, the positive effects of social capital on political participation are significantly reduced (on average leading to a 5% reduction in voter turnout).

---

[2] Note that the coefficient for the "social capital × high racial diversity" variable in column 1 of Table 5-4 is positive and statistically significant. But that does not undercut the argument regarding racial diversity's impact. The size of the coefficient is much smaller than social capital alone (see direct effects), which means that, in states with higher racial diversity, the positive effects of social capital remain but are significantly diminished. The base term for racial diversity is negative. Thus, in states with very low social capital (0), more racial diversity reduces turnout. The base term for social capital is positive. In states with no racial diversity (0), more social capital leads to higher turnout. These findings are for presidential elections; in midterm elections, the interaction term is negative. The negative effects of increased racial diversity overwhelm the positive boost in turnout from social capital in low-information midterm elections. Thus, increased social capital helps boost voter turnout more in presidential than in midterm elections.

TABLE 5-5. *Predicted Effect: Conditional Effects of Social Capital on Voter Turnout in States with High Racial Diversity*

Presidential Elections		Midterm Elections	
Level of Social Capital	VEP Turnout	Level of Social Capital	VEP Turnout
Very Low (−2SD)	50.48%	Very Low (−2SD)	43.03%
Low (−1SD)	54.02%	Low (−1SD)	43.86%
Average (mean)	57.58%	Average (mean)	44.69%
High (+1SD)	61.13%	High (+1SD)	45.52%
Very High (+2SD)	64.68%	Very High (+2SD)	46.35%
High minus low	+7%	High minus low	+2%

Note: Predicted values (probabilities) estimated with a do file in STATA. To simulate different levels of social capital, the variable was checked at its mean and then at one and two standard deviations above and below its mean. All simulations estimated for states with high racial diversity (variable set at 1). Interaction term set at (high racial diversity × level of social capital) = level of social capital. The simulations assume a senate and governor election on the ballot. All other explanatory variables were held constant at their means. Predicted values calculated from the coefficients reported in columns 2 and 3 of Table 5-3.

The second set of interactions (Table 5-5, columns 3 and 4) are calculated by multiplying the index of racial diversity by the index for social capital; again, the aim is to test the conditional effects of race and community on participation rates. The interaction term is not statistically significant in presidential elections (column 3) but is negative and statistically significant in midterm elections (column 4; this is consistent with the previous analysis regarding high-diversity states, column 2). The negative effects of racial diversity on turnout rates essentially eliminate the positive benefits of social capital in midterm elections. The reasons for this finding are unclear, but it seems to contradict the social capital thesis because we might well expect networks of social interaction (i.e., levels of social capital) to matter more, not less, in otherwise low-information elections. Of the empirical analyses conducted here, those with the interaction term are the most powerful, showing that race and social capital effects are interconnected and shape broad participation patterns in the

American states. While notable in itself, this result also suggests that the effects of racial diversity and social capital may appear to be different when considered in the aggregate than in terms of distinct racial group patterns (as indicated by our assessments in Chapter 2).

CONCLUSIONS ON STATE VOTER TURNOUT

Our evidence concerning overall turnout has reaffirmed and substantially broadened previous understanding of the importance of two contrasting influences in American politics: race and civic community. These findings shed new light by showing *that* and (perhaps more compelling) beginning to show *how* racial diversity and social capital are interrelated and affect certain aspects of politics. Direct effects of racial diversity and social capital on voter turnout rates in the states were shown, but probably more telling were revelations of the indirect and interactive (or conditional) effects of race and social capital. The magnitude of the direct effect of racial diversity on turnout is large and is similar in both midterm and presidential elections. The effect of social capital is large in presidential elections but much smaller in midterm elections, an unanticipated and somewhat puzzling finding.

The relationship between social capital and voter turnout may be partially endogenous. States with more racial diversity have lower social capital and, in turn, reduced turnout rates. The magnitude of the direct effect of social capital on voter turnout was slightly larger than the direct effect of racial diversity in presidential elections, but probability simulations demonstrated that the positive effect of social capital on turnout is also conditional on race. In states with high racial diversity, the beneficial effects of social capital on turnout rates are reduced by almost half in presidential elections and almost eliminated (2%) in midterm elections. Which of the two factors has a stronger impact individually may be important but is not easy to determine; it depends in part on which elections (presidential or midterm) are being examined. That institutional practices such as election timing may modify the effect of racial and social capital factors is also a notable finding.

Generally, this examination of political participation attests to the importance of both racial diversity and social capital – at least with regard to voter turnout. The impact of social capital seems to be minimal (or nonexistent) regarding policy outcomes or various dimensions of equality whenever racial diversity is also considered, as we have shown in previous chapters. However, social capital does have an impact on at least some indicators of participation.

INDIVIDUAL-LEVEL PARTICIPATION AND CONTEXT

The preceding analysis focused on *aggregate* state-level voter turnout; it found that both racial diversity and social capital influence participation and suggested further that the effects of social capital on voter turnout are mediated by diversity. Aggregated data alone, however, cannot be reliably used to make direct inferences about individual behavior. To further explore the relations of state racial diversity and social capital contexts to individual political behavior, we merged American National Election Studies (NES) survey data with state contextual data, measuring racial diversity by drawing on census data from appropriate years and controlling for social capital (Putnam 2000).

The NES conducts nationwide, large-scale, in-person and telephone surveys of randomly selected respondents from most of the fifty states.[3] Once again, the initial variable to be explained (dependent variable) is voting. There may be problems of

---

[3] The 1996 ANES survey includes respondents from 42 states with an average of 41 respondents per state. The 2000 NES survey include respondents from 48 of the 50 states, with a mean of 38 respondents per state. A limitation of using surveys for measuring state contextual effects is that the ANES does not sample randomly in states, but rather within geographic regions. However, similar patterns have been found using Pew surveys that do sample randomly within states (Tolbert 2005), increasing our confidence in the results reported here.

overreporting voter turnout in survey data that influence the results (Bernstein, Chadha, and Montjoy 2001, 2004). To compensate for this and – just as important – to examine *other* forms of political participation, we undertook additional analyses in which the dependent variable was an index of responses to eight political participation questions: Did the respondent vote, talk to others about candidates or parties, display buttons or signs, work for a party or candidate, attend rallies, give money to candidates, give money to parties, and/or give money to interest groups? (See Table 5-6.) Note that two of the eight items – attend political rallies and work for a political party – are also included in the measure of social and political participation (or civic equality) in Putnam's (2000) study.

The main explanatory variables considered are the overall index of state social capital (Putnam 2000, discussed earlier) and state racial diversity. For the 1996 election year, state racial context is measured by an index created for the fifty states using 1996 demographic data on the size of the African American, Latino, Asian American and Anglo populations from Current Population Surveys (Hero 1998); a similar measure is constructed from the 2000 U.S. Census. Although Putnam (2000) found the level of state social capital to be strongly associated with greater participation, its impact may prove to be diminished in a multivariate analysis that includes a measure of racial environments.

Merging the survey data with contextual data also enables us to explore other aspects of the state environments in which individuals make choices about electoral participation. At the individual level, differential voter turnout rates by socioeconomic status in American politics have long been recognized; individuals with higher income, education, and occupational status are considerably more likely to vote (Campbell et al. 1960; Wolfinger and Rosenstone 1980). We have therefore included variables measuring educational attainment (percentage of the population with at least a high-school degree), per capita income,

TABLE 5-6. *Voting in the Context of Racial Diversity and Social Capital*

Variables	1996 β (s.e.)	1996 p < |z|	2000 β (s.e.)	2000 p < |z|
State environmental variables				
Social capital	.507 (.271)	.061	.030 (.252)	.905
Racial diversity	−1.721 (.969)	.076	−1.720 (.830)	.038
Personal income per capita, 1999	−.000 (.000)	.404	.000 (.000)	.146
% high school graduates, 1999	−.038 (.035)	.288	.020 (.036)	.568
% urban, 1998	.021 (.010)	.037	−	
Republican control of state legislature, 1980–1998	−.234 (.305)	.443	−.878 (.318)	.006
Number of initiatives on the ballot	−.008 (.019)	.664	−.029 (.025)	.240
Individual-level variables				
Strong Democrat	.100 (.226)	.657	.510 (.237)	.032
Strong GOP	.022 (.242)	.927	.592 (.312)	.058
Pure Independent	−.122 (.343)	.723	−.553 (.234)	.018
Age	.004 (.005)	.397	.024 (.005)	.000
Female	.139 (.168)	.409	.291 (.165)	.079
Latino	.331 (.333)	.321	−.187 (.305)	.539
African American	−.185 (.277)	.504	.483 (.271)	.075
Education	−.012 (.058)	.836	.175 (.062)	.005
Income	.065 (.012)	.000	.057 (.028)	.045
External efficacy	.035 (.040)	.377	−.121 (.036)	.001
Political interest	.109 (.134)	.415	.356 (.062)	.000
Political knowledge	.022 (.063)	.721	.298 (.063)	.000
Discuss politics	−.037 (.037)	.326	.486 (.191)	.011
Internet access	.581 (.218)	.008	.678 (.188)	.000
TV network news	−.030 (.034)	.369	.014 (.031)	.655
Newspaper	.046 (.031)	.141	.012 (.029)	.680
Constant	2.519 (2.929)	.390	−4.675 (3.055)	.126
Pseudo R^2	.0682		.2794	
LR chi^2 (23)	69.40	.000	408.51	.000
N	930		1320	

Notes: Logistic regression coefficients; probabilities based on two-tailed test. The lack of statistically significant control variables in the 1996 NES survey has been reported in other published research and likely reflects the low-competition presidential election (Clinton's second term) that mirrors a midterm election. Hierarchical linear regression models produced similar substantive findings.

Source: 1996 and 2000 NES post-election study.

and percentage of the population that was "urban." To control for partisan effects and party control of the legislature, we used a measure of the proportion of an 19-year period (1980–1998) in which the Republican Party controlled the state legislature; this was based on data from the *Book of the States* (Tolbert and Steuernagel 2001)."[4] Previous studies show that respondents living in states with frequent exposure to ballot initiatives can be expected to report an increased probability of voting and otherwise participating in elections (Tolbert, McNeal, and Smith 2003); accordingly, we used the actual number of initiatives appearing on state election ballots in 1996 and 2000 to measure variation in state institutional environments.

An extensive literature on voter turnout has found that socio-economic factors (particularly education) and the strength of partisanship influence individual decisions on whether or not to vote (Verba and Nie 1972; Wolfinger and Rosenstone 1980; Leighley and Nagler 1992; Abramson 1983; Campbell et al. 1960; Conway 1991; Wolfinger and Rosenstone 1980; Rosenstone and Hansen 1993; Piven and Cloward 1988; Verba and Nie 1972; Verba et al. 1995). Hence, a number of variables are used to account for individual-level attitudinal and

---

[4] We used a measure of average party control of state legislatures – rather than relying on existing measures of political ideology as in the previous analysis – because the data from Erikson et al. (1993) measures policy opinions from 1976 to 1988 rather than throughout the 1980s and 1990s. The measure of state policy liberalism developed by Erikson et al. included data for 47 states whereas this variable includes data for 49 states (missing Nebraska with a unicameral legislature). The variable measures average Republican Party control of the legislature (upper and lower chambers) from 1980–1998 with raw data from the *Book of the States*. In any given year, if the Democrats controlled both houses then the state was coded 0; if the Republicans controlled both houses, the state was coded 1. If the Republicans controlled one house and the Democrats the other then the state was coded .50. If there was a tie in one house and the Democrats controlled the other house, the state was coded .25; if there was a tie in one house and the Republicans controlled the other, the state was coded .75. Data for the years 1980–1998 was summed and then divided by the number of years analyzed. If a state (such as Colorado) is coded 1 in the final index, then the Republican party has controlled both houses of the legislature every session for the past 19 years. If a state is coded .20, the Republican Party has controlled the legislature for 20% of the 1980–1998 period. If a state (such as California) is coded .05, then the Republican Party has controlled the legislature for only 5% of the 1980–1998 period.

demographic factors (see Lewis-Beck and Rice 1992; Wolfinger and Rosenstone 1980) as follows. Partisanship is measured on a 7-point scale, with possible responses ranging from 1 = strong Democrat to 7 = strong Republican; a series of dummy variables are used to account for political attitudes – including strong Democrat, strong Republican, and pure Independent – with weak partisans as the reference group. We account for education (measured on a 7-point scale) as well as gender (using a binary variable for female respondent). To control for ethnic background, respondents were coded 1 if African American or Latino and 0 otherwise. Another potentially important variable is age (measured in years). Because discussing politics with friends and family is an important source of political information, we included an ordinal variable measuring the frequency of political discussions with family and friends.

To account for information consumption, we used data on how many days (during the previous week) the respondent read the newspaper and watched the national nightly news. Because the Internet has become a significant avenue for political information and has been shown to increase voter turnout, we also included a variable coded 1 for Internet access and 0 otherwise was used (Tolbert and McNeal 2003; cf. Norris 2001; Bimber 2003; Mossberger, Tolbert, and Stansbury 2003). Political interest is an important predictor of voting, and is measured using a scale ranging from very much interested in the campaign to not much interested. To control for "external efficacy" or confidence in government responsiveness, we combined the response scores to two statements – "People don't have say in government" and "Public officials don't care about people like me" – into a 5-point scale ranging from strongly disagree to strongly agree. The final control variable is for political knowledge, measured by the number of six general political questions correctly answered.[5]

---

[5] In 1996 the questions were: What position does Al Gore hold? What position does William Rehnquist hold? What position does Boris Yeltsin hold? What position does

FINDINGS

Voting in Context

The dependent variable in Table 5-6 is coded so that higher scores are associated with increased likelihood of voting. (Since the dependent variable is binary, logistic regression coefficients are reported.) Columns 1 and 2 report findings from the 1996 and 2000 NES data, respectively.

A remarkable finding in Table 5-6 is that state racial diversity is a statistically significant predictor of voting in both of the presidential elections (1996 and 2000); thus, state racial diversity has a direct effect on individual voter turnout when context is considered. This is consistent with previous research (Hill and Leighley 1999). In states with high racial diversity, citizens are significantly less likely to vote in presidential elections, even after we control for a battery of individual and state environmental factors. Diversity is the most consistent predictor of voting of all the state environmental variables and the only one to be statistically significant in both election years. *Ceteris paribus*, citizens in states with high social capital were more likely to vote in 1996, but social capital was not statistically related to an increased probability of voting in 2000 once racial diversity was taken into account. This indicates a more consistent effect for the context of racial diversity context than of social capital.

Other Forms of Political Participation

Although voting is clearly a fundamental political act, it is but one form of participation. To more fully examine the relation

Newt Gingrich hold? Which party had a majority in the House before the election? Which party had a majority in the Senate before the election? In 2000 the questions were: What position does Trent Lott hold? What position does William Rehnquist hold? What position does Tony Blair hold? What position does Janet Reno hold? Which party had a majority in the House before the election? Which party had a majority in the Senate before the election?

of racial diversity and social capital to political participation, we examined the survey data using an index of responses to eight political participation questions as the dependent variable; the results are reported in Table 5-7, columns 1 and 2 for the 1996 and 2000 elections (respectively). When the idea of political participation is expanded to include more than just voting, the impact of state racial diversity is even more pronounced.

In both 1996 and 2000, respondents in states with higher racial diversity were significantly less likely to participate in various political acts. The statistically significant and negative relationship with the participation index was evident even after we controlled for extensive individual and state contextual factors associated with political participation. Furthermore, when racial diversity is considered in the analyses, social capital was *not* a significant predictor concerning the index of political participation in either of the years examined. Respondents in states with higher social capital were not more likely to participate politically in either the 1996 or the 2000 election year. This suggests that state racial diversity has a more significant and perhaps broader impact in explaining various forms of political participation than does a state's score on the social capital index (Putnam 2000). The data provide, then, considerable evidence that state racial diversity context is associated with political participation in America. However, other contextual factors of socioeconomic influence – particularly social capital but also income, education, and urbanization – are not. The impact of racial diversity is notable even if expected, but the *absence* of impact of the other contextual variables is striking.

The index of political participation is useful, but it is instructive also to examine the relationship between social capital, racial diversity, and each of the different forms of participation separately. Different forms of participation vary with respect to the time required, the nature and extent of interpersonal relations or contacts, monetary investment, and other dimensions. We examined (but do not present in table form) the responses

TABLE 5-7. *Participation Index in the Context of Racial Diversity and Social Capital*

Variables	1996 β (s.e.)	1996 p < |z|	2000 β (s.e.)	2000 p < |z|
State environmental variables				
Social capital	.050 (.091)	.584	−.063 (.064)	.330
Racial diversity index	−.536 (.320)	.095	−488 (.235)	.038
Personal income per capita, 1999	.000 (.000)	.664	−.000 (.000)	.937
% high-school graduates, 1999	−.006 (.011)	.552	.011 (.010)	.274
% urban, 1998	.002 (.003)	.569	−	
Republican control of state legislature, 1980–1998	.030 (.094)	.748	−.086 (.088)	.329
Number of initiatives on ballot	.008 (.006)	.180	−.003 (.007)	.592
Individual-level variables				
Strong Democrat	.050 (.072)	.485	.160 (.059)	.007
Strong GOP	.211 (.071)	.003	.138 (.065)	.034
Pure Independent	−.029 (.130)	.818	−.265 (.100)	.008
Age	.003 (.001)	.094	.004 (.001)	.010
Female	−.033 (.055)	.546	−.015 (.048)	.751
Latino	−.010 (.117)	.928	−.002 (.102)	.978
African America	−.085 (.109)	.434	.020 (.086)	.816
Education	.041 (.018)	.029	.020 (.017)	.252
Income	.005 (.004)	.250	.017 (.006)	.006
External efficacy	.020 (.013)	.126	−.031 (.010)	.004
Political interest	.233 (.045)	.000	.157 (.021)	.000
Political knowledge	.022 (.022)	.313	.046 (.017)	.007
Discuss politics	.039 (.011)	.001	.418 (.084)	.000
Internet access	.087 (.063)	.169	.145 (.060)	.017
TV network news	−.009 (.011)	.392	.002 (.009)	.813
Newspaper	.015 (.010)	.149	.011 (.008)	.181
Constant	−.442 (.974)	.650	−1.796 (.863)	.037
Pseudo R^2	.0533		.1064	
LR chi² (23)	149.69	.000	424.59	.000
N	928		1318	

Notes: Negative binomial regression coefficients; probabilities based on two-tailed test. Hierarchical linear regression models produced similar substantive findings.

Source: 1996 and 2000 NES post-election study.

to the seven political participation questions – using logistic regression while controlling for an extensive range of demographic variables. Respondents in states with high social capital were not more likely to participate in *any* of the seven activities. State social capital was *not* a significant predictor of these other forms of political participation, including "attending political rallies" and "working for a political party," which were parts of the participation index used in some social capital studies (Putnam 2000). In states with high racial diversity, individuals were significantly *less* likely to participate in five of the seven political activities. These are especially notable findings because we would expect social capital to be as or more important (but certainly not less so) in these various nonelectoral forms of participation. The data again suggest that a state's racial diversity context is an important predictor of political behavior; social capital is much less so (if at all) after various other factors are accounted for.

CONCLUSION

Some political scholars firmly claim that social capital enhances civic engagement and political participation in the United States, and indeed empirical studies (Putnam 2000) on the subject and some of the analysis in this chapter have provided support for this claim. Some evidence in this chapter assuredly supports that assertion, especially with regard to aggregate indicators of voting. However, social capital does not always have a consistent and major effect on participation, especially when other factors are taken into account; social capital's impact varies as a function of (i) the type of the election, presidential or midterm; (ii) whether one examines aggregate turnout alone versus taking context into account; and (iii) what type of participation is considered. In virtually every instance, it seems social capital's impact on participation is conditioned by the degree of racial diversity. On the other hand, it seems that racial diversity matters fairly consistently with respect to participation (Hero 1998; Hill and Leighley 1999). Diversity has both a direct and an indirect effect on voter turnout, whereas social capital may be only an endogenous explanation of voter turnout that is actually rooted in levels of racial diversity. The interactive effects we examined were particularly interesting and suggest roles for both social capital and diversity, with the latter being somewhat more influential. Moreover, our analysis of survey data based on two recent presidential elections lends little support to the notion that social capital itself has a positive direct impact on various forms of political participation once racial diversity is accounted for. We observe that the context of racial diversity seems to affect individual forms of participation other than voting yet the same cannot be said of social capital.

To be appropriately cautious, it should be stressed that we examined data consisting of a somewhat different set of indicators of participation than did the major social capital study (Putnam 2000). Here, electoral-related participation – voting and campaign-related activities – has been the focus of analysis. Although he considers some similar activities and frequently refers to "political" participation, overall Putnam (see pp. 497, 359) focuses most often on what might more accurately be construed as essentially "civic" or volunteering or social activities: served as an officer of some club or organization, attended a public meeting on town or school affairs, signed a petition, made a speech, wrote a letter to the newspaper, wrote an article for a magazine or newspaper, was a member of some "better government" group, held or ran for political office. Some research suggests these activities may carry over to other arenas of politics, including electoral participation (Verba et al. 1995), but that is not consistently evident in the present study. Hence the different dependent variables used may partly explain the differing results.

Aggregate and individual participation are sometimes – but not always – greater in higher social capital contexts after we take a state's ethnic composition into account. Individuals within contexts of high minority diversity are less likely to vote or participate in politics (Hill and Leighley 1999; Hero 1998). Again, the impact of social capital on participation is almost always racially contingent.

6

Public Policy Outputs

A major goal of democratic politics is to create social conditions such that people can "enjoy better lives" (Radcliff 2001). Democratic politics is certainly affected by its "civil society" – its societal, informal elements – as social capital arguments emphasize. But formal governmental institutions and public policies are clearly important as well, and they most often are presumed to reflect and complement a democratic polity's civil society. Social conditions are not simply "a given": they are potentially alterable and can vary significantly across and even within political systems. As is evident from the earlier chapters in this book, there is substantial variation in the social and political conditions of the fifty American states. The central question in this chapter is: Are political jurisdictions (here, the states) that have more social capital *also* the ones that adopt basic public (governmental) policies that advance social conditions consistent with essential values of equality? Specifically, were American states with higher social capital more likely to adopt civil rights policies (before the federal legislation of the 1960s) and more likely to have tax policies that are not regressive; and do they provide more in the way of welfare policy benefits? Does racial diversity matter on these questions?

More generally, This chapter considers the public policy choices or out*puts* of governments rather than the social out*comes* typically examined in studies of social capital and racial diversity (Hero 1998). Is a state's (informal) "social infrastructure" (Putnam 2000, p. 298) or social capital – which allegedly influences its sense of equality and degree of "well-being" – associated with corresponding (formal, governmental) policy efforts? What is the relationship between civil society and the state? Are salutary outcomes essentially spillovers of civic associational orientations and activities? Are governmental policies an extension of, a complement to, a substitute for, or perhaps even unrelated to social capital? And now does racial diversity affect the answers to these questions?

The constitutional design of America's liberal democracy embodies a particular approach toward the achievement of broad social goals – which includes "promoting the general welfare" – that is structured to adequately empower yet also to constrain governmental actions. A central element in that design is federalism; this affirms that state governments have critical roles in defining and seeking to achieve various social purposes, which means that states are fundamental polities in and of themselves. Furthermore, federalism allows and expects that states will vary in their social conditions and in their governmental initiatives to address and perhaps improve those conditions.

As emphasized in earlier chapters, a wide range of salutary outcomes in the American states have been attributed to higher levels of social capital. Analyses of social capital's impact on social outcomes are emphatically clear and powerful in their conclusions: higher levels of social capital are strongly related to an array of beneficial social outcomes. Recall that with respect to various social outcomes – child welfare, educational performance, safe and productive neighborhoods, economic prosperity, and health and happiness – higher levels of social capital are strongly related to "better" outcomes (Putnam 2000). More specifically, it is found that: "kids are better off in high social capital states," "schools work better in high social capital states," "health is better in high social capital states," and, furthermore, "social capital and tolerance go together" (Putnam 2000, p. 356). Additionally, social capital is found to be strongly related to both economic and civic equality.

While acknowledging the notable findings in Putnams landmark study (*Bowling Alone*) of social capital, some authors have criticized the thesis (see, e.g., Theiss-Morse and Hibbing 2005; Putzel 1997). In Chapter 4 we demonstrated that social capital's impact on social outcomes is substantially diminished or nonexistent (sometimes even reversed) when racial/ethnic factors are considered (see also Hero 2003a); in other words, it is racial diversity rather than social capital that primarily explains a number of those outcomes. But another issue – the one to be examined in this chapter – is that the social capital thesis scarcely recognizes (much less seeks to account for) the impact of formal governmental institutions and practices, including public policies or outputs (see, e.g., Lowndes and Wilson 2001).

The implication of social capital studies is that social capital has a fundamental and pervasive effect on social relations and the broader social and political system. However, in addition to the research cited previously (Hero 1998; Hero 2003a) various scholars have questioned this "transmission belt" view of civil society, the notion that "the beneficial formative effects" of social capital "spill over from one sphere to another," that is, from the civic to other spheres (Rosenblum 1998, p. 48; Theiss-Morse and Hibbing 2005). Whether social capital's impact carries over to the governmental domain has not been systematically examined in research on U.S. public policy. Social capital's emphasis is overwhelmingly on civic association as the central explanation of general social well-being. Accordingly, it could reasonably be inferred that government actions are not seen as particularly important since government ("the state") receives little attention in these studies. Social well-being is found to be at its greatest when civic association and informal civic engagement is at high levels (and when that engagement embodies "bridging" rather than "bonding" activities – Putnam 2000). But there is virtual silence regarding government and welfare and other policy (at least in most social capital analyses of the United States).

There appears to be something of a grudging acceptance of a role for government or formal institutions within the leading social capital studies. For example, Putnam (2000, p. 147) states: "For better or worse, we rely increasingly – we are forced to rely increasingly – on formal institutions, and above all on the law, to accomplish what we used to accomplish through informal networks reinforced by generalized reciprocity – that is, through social capital." Except to suggest that increases in public policies hasten the decline of social capital through "displacement," social capital analyses seldom take up the question of what relationship there might be between the two. Some studies have assessed the relation of social capital to government "performance" (Rice and Sumberg 1997) and government "accountability" (Knack 2002). However, the dependent variables examined in those studies are different, and the measurement of social capital varies from what we take to be the authoritative study of social capital (i.e., Putnam 2000); there are also various other differences between those studies and the present one, including the set of independent variables considered and how some of them are measured.

The most prominent social capital arguments suggest that there are troubling implications associated with the increased reliance on formal versus informal methods of pursuing social goals (Putnam 2000). But this raises a question: When formal public policies regarding aspects of basic fairness and general well-being *are* adopted, do they follow a pattern that is in any way related to the levels of social capital? Do different levels of social capital in a society translate into parallel *formal* public policies?

Social capital studies have generally provided little specific guidance on what to expect regarding a relationship between levels of social capital and the public policy inclinations of the American states (see Rice and Sumberg 1997). They have emphasized the association of social capital to civic equality, economic equality, and tolerance among a host of better social outcomes. Given social capital's arguments about equality, it seems that we might reasonably anticipate a stronger orientation toward civil rights as well as basic "fairness" in raising revenues that support governmental activity. It might also be expected that there would be greater formal welfare support or generosity in contexts of higher social capital – at least once the resources of civil society are deemed insufficient and the necessity of seeking government action has been determined in the first place. There are additional reasons to anticipate that more extensive equitable policies would occur in high–social capital contexts.

Some years prior to the publication of *Bowling Alone*, Robert Putnam suggested that "social capital is not a substitute for effective public policy" and that social capital is both a "prerequisite" for effective public policy and, "in part, a consequence of it." Furthermore, "wise policy can encourage social capital formation, and social capital itself enhances the effectiveness of government action" (Putnam 1993, as quoted in Putzel 1997, p. 948).

It is not clear whether this is meant to suggest that the implementation or the very formulation of public policy were aided by social capital, but it may be so. What Putnam meant by "effective" policy is not obvious, and neither is the substantive content of policies that would be seen to accord with social capital arguments. Furthermore, the direction of causality – policy to social capital or vice versa – is ambiguous. However, higher social capital would seem to be at least associated with more "positive" public policies.

In his study of social capital assessing the quality and performance of U.S. state governments' "management practices," Knack (2002) argues that "social capital can broaden government accountability, so that government must be responsive to citizens at large rather than to narrow interests" – that is, government is responsive to "broader interests" in higher–social capital settings (p. 773; see also Chapter 2 herein). Furthermore, social capital has been shown to be strongly related to the categories of "political culture," a concept developed by Daniel Elazar (1984). In fact, according to, Putnam: "The correlation between the political-culture index derived from Elazar's study and our Social Capital index is strikingly large"; the inter-state differences in levels of social capital "are astonishingly similar to differences in 'state political culture' as drawn from the 1950s by political historian Daniel Elazar" (Putnam 2000, pp. 346–7, 294). Contexts where there are high levels of social capital especially coincide with Elazar's "moralistic" political culture, according some previous research (Hero 1998, 2003b). "In the moralistic political culture" there is "a general commitment to utilizing communal – preferably non-governmental, but governmental if necessary – power to intervene into the sphere of private activities when it is considered necessary to do so *for the public good or the well-being of the community*. By virtue of its fundamental outlook, the moralistic culture creates a greater commitment to active government intervention in the economic and social life of the community" (Elazar 1984, pp. 117–8, emphasis added). It was also argued that the moralistic culture helped explain more expansive civil rights policies in the states during the 1960s and a more egalitarian orientation in general (p. 196); others assert that culture also embodies a concern for equality of "results" (Hanson 1994), not only equal opportunity.

Clearly, then, numerous previous social capital (and political culture) empirical studies provide firm ground for us to anticipate more equality when there is high social capital (but see Hero 2003a). The relation of social capital and sense of community – civil society – to better general social outcomes and well-being seems well established in that body of research (Putnam 2000; Elazar 1984; cf. Hero 1998, 2003a). But whether there is a relationship between social capital and the formal public policies of state governments in the United States has not been examined.

Yet this should be done in order to more fully understand the impacts of social capital and racial diversity in fostering policies that are conducive to better social conditions (cf. Theiss-Morse and Hibbing 2005).

In this chapter I consider civil rights, tax policy, and welfare policy vis-à-vis social capital and racial diversity, because these policies address issues associated with matters of basic procedural rights, fairness, and general well-being and thus are all linked to values of equality. These policies – and particularly the first two (civil rights and tax progressivity) – are useful in that they arguably address basic *principles* of procedural equality and fairness rather than the more normatively contentious issues of contemporary liberal versus conservative public policy orientations. In this regard I differ from other studies by examining policies that are not necessarily meant to "reflect the usual ideological divisions between liberals and conservatives" (Rice and Sumberg 1977). Elazar had also argued that political cultures were *neither* synonymous with nor substitutes for "liberal" and "conservative" ideological orientations. And there is little in Putnam's *Bowling Alone* to suggest that there is (or is expected to be) much of an association between levels of social capital and specific ideological orientations.

This emphasis on basic procedural equality and issues of fairness is patently appropriate for civil rights legislation, although we know well that the adoption of such policies by the federal government was highly controversial. For our examination of tax policy, observe that the measure used does *not* imply that either lower or higher levels of government taxation is better. Nor am I arguing (for present purposes) that "progressive" taxes are better than flat-rate taxes, although the logic of social capital and related arguments suggest that regressive tax systems are questionable because they foster inequality. (Note that all but seven states had some degree of regressive tax policies in 1990.) Our indicator of tax progressivity is meant to assess only the "fairness" of state policies in raising revenues, whatever level of revenues those might be.

Welfare policy may differ in important respects from the previous two issues because, as a clearly redistributive policy, it has been viewed as a leading example of liberal versus conservative ideology in the United States. Even so, Elazar and others have argued that we should not be surprised to find that political culture (Elazar 1984; Gray 1999; Rom 1996) and "civic culture" (Rice and Sumberg 1997) affect public policies, including welfare. But few if any of these studies have included racial diversity in their analyses. On the other hand, much historical and institutional research has shown how racial considerations shaped the very formation and development of American welfare policy, including the degree to which states have been granted discretion in implementing welfare policy. Moreover, a considerable body of work has demonstrated the strong and consistent effect of racial composition on states' welfare policy decisions in the aftermath of the "reform legislation" (in 1996) that granted even more discretion to states than they previously had (see Chapter 3). Although this research has taken into account a number of variables in addition to racial diversity, social capital has generally not been among those variables. Thus, research embodying each of the two interpretations – social capital and racial diversity – have examined welfare as an important policy, but they have usually done so separately: including one but not the other. This means that considering the two perspectives jointly is a valuable line of inquiry for our study.

At the outset, it should be acknowledged that the evidence drawn upon here is at times indirect and is not as firm as we would like; the evidence is more suggestive than definitive. However, the issues addressed seem important enough to be explored as best we can. It is hoped that this exploration will encourage later research on similar matters.

CIVIL RIGHTS

The latter half of the twentieth century was one of fundamental change in the American polity. The 1950s featured landmark

Supreme Court cases; the 1960s witnessed enactment of the Civil Rights Act (1964), the Voting Rights Act (1965), and open housing legislation (1968). These policies typically centered on procedural equality and equality of opportunity, but the War on Poverty, focused on economic equality. There was, in addition, the enactment of major immigration legislation (1965) as well as the emergence of policies based on racial criteria (affirmative action) and what came to be called "multicultural" policies, including bilingual education (1967) and election ballots (1975). Together, these various policies have been characterized as part of a "minority rights revolution" (Skrentny 2002). A common thread influencing support for civil rights in the 1960s was concern over America's international exigencies, particularly the Cold War, and its status as a defender and advocate of racial equality (Klinkner and Smith 1999; Skrentny 2002). Viewed from the racial diversity perspective, it is notable that the prevailing, generally high levels of social capital in the pre–civil rights era (Putnam 2000) seemed not to have much impact on procedural equality policies. That is, the emergence of civil rights was in some substantial part attributable to external factors (the Cold War) and to the efforts of civil rights activists to apply basic (liberal) freedom without discrimination based on race; the significance of high social capital in the states is not evident in accounts of the era (e.g., Schattschneider 1960).

Civil rights, voting rights, and fair housing legislation were intended to eliminate discrimination against racial minorities, especially blacks, as efforts to extend or provide procedural equality and rights often focused on the removal and prohibition of certain discriminatory behaviors. That is, these were policies that concerned the nondiscriminatory access to (or enforcement of) the traditional civil and political rights of citizenship for all, with specific attention to the individual members of minority groups. The policies did not have explicit redistributive goals as such, although in light of long-standing conditions the policies' implications were enormous both symbolically and substantively. One important example is that, prior to various judicial decrees of the 1960s mandating eligibility of blacks for policy benefits, "some states, particularly those in the Deep South, administered welfare programs almost solely for whites" (Albritton 1990, p. 422). Thus, in addition to its direct and manifest purposes, civil rights legislation had the effect of increasing minority access to substantive *existing* policy benefits. Yet the increased presence of blacks among welfare recipients – brought about by applying civil rights policies to the implementation of welfare – generated strong reactions against welfare (see, e.g., Gilens 2003). Indeed, Gilens argues that following the mandated black eligibility for welfare in the mid-1960s, welfare policy became highly "racialized." Hence, to some degree civil rights and welfare became intertwined and probably cannot be understood separately from one another (cf. Skrentny 2002). The temporal coincidence of this racialization of welfare policy and the "collapse of social capital" (Putnam 2000) is striking.

Previous research has examined adoption of civil rights policies in the states during the 1960s. According to Dye, the civil rights policies of the states – as he measured them – regarding state adoption and implementation of fair employment, fair housing, and open accommodations legislation (Dye 1969, p. 1089; see also Lockard 1968, pp. 21–2) – were linked to states' racial composition as well as to economic development. Larger nonwhite populations were associated with the adoption of less extensive civil rights policies, and greater economic development was associated with more extensive policies. Other writers have likewise pointed to the importance of racial diversity while noting also the importance of other factors, such as "political culture." Regarding state antidiscrimination laws of the early 1960s (including public accommodations, employment, public and public-assisted housing, private housing, and education) and based on data from U.S. Civil Rights Commission Report of 1962, Elazar (1984, pp. 168–9) argued that "it was a combination of the moralistic political culture plus the existence of a high degree of ethnic diversity that led to this kind of legislation. The affected ethnics, in effect, challenged the majority to live up to the demand of their political culture and virtually embarrass[ed] them into doing so."

Although Elazar's tone is assertive in this claim, the actual evidence he offered was impressionistic and did not include a systematic assessment of civil rights and political culture. Furthermore, his claim also overlooked that there were very few if any states with "moralistic political culture plus the existence of a high degree of ethnic diversity" (as demonstrated in the present study and elsewhere; see Hero 1998).

Using data from Dye (1969), I examined the relationship between states' civil rights scores and the social capital index (Putnam 2000). One must acknowledge that there is something of a time mismatch in that the civil rights scores (from the mid-1960s) and the social capital index (from the mid-1970s to mid-1990s) are from different periods. (However, *Bowling Alone* implies there has been long-term stability in the relative ranking of states' social capital.) Exercising appropriate caution while interpreting the findings, it can be noted that the simple correlation between the civil rights scores and the social capital index is quite weak: only .31. When other factors are accounted for, including diversity and several socioeconomic factors, the relationship between social capital and civil rights drops to insignificance.

Clear limitations of the data notwithstanding, the evidence is more consistent with Dye's (and the diversity) argument that race played a leading role in explaining states' civil rights policies in the era before the federal government's major policy adoptions. As far as one can tell with this admittedly qualified evidence, social capital per se appears unrelated to the civil rights policies of the states in the 1960s, undercutting the social capital argument; in contrast, the racial diversity thesis receives support.

TAX POLICY

To examine tax policies I relied on regressivity scores, which "represent the percentage of income extracted in taxes from the lowest 40 percent of income earners as a percentage of the percent of income extracted from the top 5 percentage of income earners in each state" (Winters 1999). A score of 100 signifies proportionality; scores below 100 signify progressive tax policies and those above 100 indicate regressiveness.

Some states with high social capital (among the top 10 on the social capital index) and low racial diversity – such as Vermont (87), Montana (99), and Minnesota (101) – indeed have progressive or essentially proportional tax systems. But other states with among the highest levels of social capital (in the top 10) have quite regressive tax systems. North Dakota has the highest level of social capital, yet scores 172 on regressivity; more striking, South Dakota has the second-highest level of social capital and scores 308. Washington (with the tenth-highest level) scores 326, New Hampshire (sixth-highest) scores 215, and Wyoming (ninth-highest) scores 258. At the same time, some states with low social capital score better than a number of top-10 social capital states. For example, North Carolina and South Carolina, both in the bottom 10 on social capital, each scores 117 on regressivity – clearly better than the Dakotas, Washington, New Hampshire, and Wyoming (Winters 1999, p. 316).

The findings for tax policy and social capital are depicted in Figure 6-1. The overall distribution shows no significant (statistical) relation between states' social capital and tax policy. This echoes previous research findings that "political culture" (Elazar 1984) has no impact on tax progressivity or negressivity noted in Hero 1998, p. 111). Thus, for a direct indicator of an egalitarian dimension of state policy, social capital (and political culture) is irrelevant.

It must be noted, however, that the impact of racial diversity on tax policy also appears to be virtually nonexistent. Thus, for the crucial matter of tax fairness, *neither* of the two analytical perspectives provides any insight to speak of. Perhaps the most that can be said is that, whatever level of regressiveness there is in a state's tax system, racial minorities are

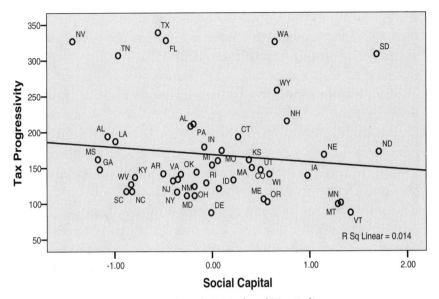

FIGURE 6-1. Social Capital and Tax Policy

almost certainly disproportionately affected since they are disproportionately represented among lower income levels across the states and in the United States as a whole.

WELFARE

Next we examine welfare policy. As noted, it is not clear whether social capital theorists would think it legitimate to consider welfare policy when assessing the theory's core claims. To complicate matters further, there are rather different views among policy scholars concerning what aspects and associated measures are the appropriate ones for an examination of states' welfare policies. For example, Albritton (1990, pp. 426–7) lists a number of ways that welfare policy has been measured: (1) state welfare expenditure per $1,000 personal income; (2) welfare as a percentage of total state expenditures; (3) number of recipients per 1,000 population; (4) adequacy of welfare assistance grants (ratio of grants to per capita income); and (5) adequacy of welfare grants plus food stamp value in relation to per capita income. Other studies have included measures of expenditures per recipient and cash benefit levels.

It is difficult to draw conclusions about the impact of social capital (Putnam 2000) on welfare based on the five measures listed by Albritton. For instance, in 1985 North Dakota (first in social capital) ranked 20th, 38th, 47th, 11th, and 12th on the five indicators while South Dakota (second in social capital) ranked 38th, 37th, 42nd, 22nd, and 19th. Contrasting, somewhat were Vermont (third in social capital), which ranked 6th, 15th, 18th, 4th, and 4th; and Minnesota (fourth in social capital), which ranked 9th, 11th, 26th, 3rd, and 7th. In short, there is much variation and no clearly consistent effect of social capital on these different indicators. But there are other ways to measure welfare policy, one of which we consider next.

An often-used measure of welfare is "cash benefit levels," which indicates the maximum cash benefits for a family of three. Cash benefit levels are seen as providing one of the most visible and valid policy indicators of welfare benefit generosity that are under the control of state governments (Rom 2004, Plotnick and Winters 1985). However useful this indicator may be, states do not necessarily provide payments that meet these levels; the maximum is the maximum that *can* be received, but this is not necessarily the amount actually received. Bearing this important caveat in mind, we examined cash benefits for several years – 1985, 1990, 1995, and 1999 – in relation to social capital. These data may appear to pose a problem in that the welfare variables change over time while the social capital indicator does not. However, the data used by Putnam to create the social capital index are aggregated primarily over the period of the mid-1970s to mid-1990s (see Putnam 2000, p. 435), and thus largely coincide in time with the welfare benefits examined here. Putnam's indicator of social capital was also, of course, the linchpin of his empirical analysis and of the numerous substantive and theoretical claims he advanced. Moreover, Putnam argues (as do other scholars), that social capital is quite stable over time (cf. Elazar's

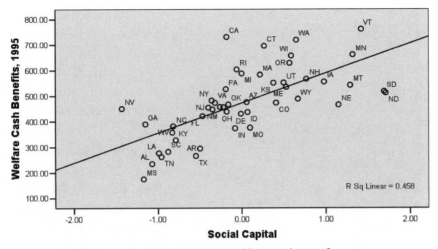

FIGURE 6-2. Social Capital and Welfare Cash Benefits, 1995

1984 parallel claims about "political culture"); indeed, the very concept of culture implies reasonably long-term continuity. And assessing the relationships at several distinct times, as we do here, should increase confidence in the findings that emerge.

The relationship of social capital to welfare cash benefit level is shown in the scatterplots of Figures 6-2 and 6-3. The 1995 data in Figure 6-2 suggest a strong positive relationship between social capital and welfare cash benefits in that year; and the patterns for 1995 are quite similar to (although slightly stronger than) those in 1990 and 1985. In short, there is substantial evidence of a strong association between social capital and welfare cash benefits. Furthermore, this association holds up even after controlling for other factors, including racial diversity. So even though social capital analyses do not always focus on policy outputs, this evidence on welfare policy seems consistent with the spirit of social capital claims. However, compare Figure 6-3, showing data for 1999, which is in strong and perhaps surprising contrast to Figure 6-2: it indicates no relationship at all between social capital and welfare benefit cash levels.

As suggested by the scatterplots (and as shown also by data analysis), the correlation between social capital and welfare cash benefit levels becomes nonexistent in 1999 – that is, *after* the

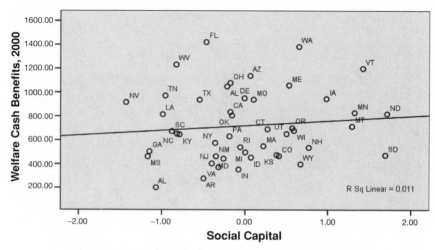

FIGURE 6-3. Social Capital and Welfare Cash Benefits, 2000

welfare reform legislation of 1996. That legislation, Temporary Assistance for Needy Families (TANF), gave the states greater discretion over welfare policy in some important respects (summarized in Rom 1999, p. 322; but see Soss et al. 2001). Under TANF, in comparison to the pre-reform policies of Aid to Families with Dependent Children (AFDC), the states "have much more power.... The states can determine who is eligible for TANF, what obligations they face and what benefits they receive, and how the programs will be designed, implemented, and evaluated." Second, AFDC "was an entitlement to individuals and TANF is not. The federal government gives each state a block of funds to pay for the program each year. . . . The states can use a substantial portion of their TANF funds for purposes other than providing cash benefits."

Rom adds that another important difference between the post- and pre-reform legislation is that "the main goal of TANF is to promote work, not provide income support to poor families [as did AFDC]." Also, "TANF is much more concerned with changing recipient behavior than was AFDC" (Rom 2004, p. 323). For instance, states were given greater discretion to adopt policies that were perceived as discouraging recipients' "dependency"; the new legislation allowed states to cut off benefits earlier than the five years suggested by federal law. States could also try to "discourage childbearing" by denying "benefits to unmarried teenagers and their children or to children born while their mothers were receiving benefits" (Rom 2004, p. 323).

It is interesting that, after states were given *greater* discretion over welfare eligibility and after it was no longer an entitlement, the relationship between social capital and welfare benefit levels disappears; when states had somewhat less discretion this relationship seems to have been rather strong. We would have expected the reverse to hold, given that the impact of such factors as social capital should be stronger when states are less restrained by "external" (federal government) directives, but that seems not to be the case. We are not sure what could explain the previously strong (from 1980 to the mid-1990s) and the subsequently (post-1995) nonexistent relationship between social capital and welfare benefit levels. Some have argued that the pejorative depiction of welfare – combined with the racial and social class connotation embodied in the "welfare queen" notion was critical in gaining support for welfare "reform" (Hancock 2004). In any case, the social capital–welfare cash benefit level relation that once existed was never evident in other measures or dimensions of welfare policy.

It has been previously shown that not only cash benefit levels but also other aspects of welfare policy are affected by the racial composition of states (Howard 1999); recall also that the size of a state's minority population has been shown to be inversely related to social capital (Hero 2003a). To quickly restate points made earlier (see Chapter 3): larger racial minority group presence is associated with less extensive welfare policies (Johnson 2001, 2003), and the direct and indirect effects of this were evident in both the pre– and post–welfare reform periods (i.e., before and after 1996). These findings led Johnson to conclude that "it appears that policymakers have a different relationship with the racial majority in their states than with the racial minority: They *respond* to whites and *react* to the presence of African Americans" (2003, pp. 161–3, emphasis in original). Other analyses of welfare policy in the post-welfare reform period have further underscored the importance of race in the formulation and implementation stages of welfare policy.

Higher percentages of African Americans on state welfare rolls were related to stricter sanctions, stricter time limits, and family caps. In addition, states with higher percentages of Latino recipients tended to have stricter time limits and family caps. Moreover, higher percentages of the two groups tended to negatively affect benefit levels (Soss et al. 2001). Another analysis (Fellowes and Rowe 2004) reaffirms these earlier findings regarding "the strong role of race in TANF politics," as seen in three dimensions of the policy: stricter rules governing initial eligibility, less flexibility in new welfare work requirements, and lower cash benefits to welfare recipients. A negative relationship between the percentage of welfare recipients who are Latino and cash benefit levels has also been identified.

An analysis of the implementation dimension of TANF policy through a case study (Keiser et al. 2004) found that "sanction rates increase as the nonwhite population increases." (This pattern changes, however, when African Americans are the majority.) Hence, this study of post-reform welfare policy focused on another aspect – implementation – and affirms the significance of race in generally dampening welfare policies that had been found in previous studies.

CONCLUSIONS

This chapter engaged questions concerning whether public policies or governmental *outputs*, as distinct from social *outcomes*, are affected by social capital and/or racial diversity. The principal social capital studies of the United States have not addressed these questions and provide little guidance concerning what to expect. Nonetheless, it seems that certain expectations could be reasonably inferred, and we observed that comments by scholars of social capital (Putnam 1993) and political culture (Elazar 1984) were consistent with those inferences (also see Rice and

Sumberg 1997; Knack 2002). That is, one would expect that social capital is associated with policies that support and advance equality in various ways; yet racial diversity arguments suggest essentially the reverse. We deemed three types of outputs – civil rights, tax policy ("fairness"), and welfare – to be appropriate and important enough to warrant further examination.

Racial diversity was shown to have substantial (negative) impacts on states' civil rights policies (Dye 1969), while (positive) impacts of social capital appeared at most minimal. When examined alone with respect to states' civil rights policies in the 1960s, the impact of social capital is weak; when other factors are accounted for (in multivariate analysis) its impact essentially disappears. Hence basic legal principles of equality seem *not* to have been consistently more common in states with higher levels of social capital before the federal civil rights legislation of the mid-1960s. In terms of the basic fairness of state tax systems – that is, how regressive, proportional, or progressive those systems are – social capital has no impact whatsoever, though neither does racial diversity in the aggregate.

Welfare policy presents a more complicated picture. There is a considerable body of research indicating the importance of race on states' welfare policies in both the pre- and post-1996 welfare reform periods. Such effects have been manifest as much in eligibility and sanction requirements as in expenditures. Social capital was shown to have had a significant effect on at least one measure of welfare policy, maximum cash benefit levels for a family of three – for a number of years leading up to the 1996 reform legislation. However, in the post-reform period the significance of social capital for cash benefit levels vanishes, which is a puzzling and unexpected finding. The racialization of gender also plays a role in understanding the reform policies (Hancock 2004). Firm conclusions about social capital's influence on welfare policy are hard to reach, however.

On balance, there appears to be more evidence in support of the diversity than the social capital thesis. Racial diversity's impact on the adoption of civil rights policies is considerable, and the theory is supported by various findings with regard to welfare. The social capital thesis, on the other hand, receives limited support at most. There is scant evidence of an independent effect of social capital on early civil rights policies and no relationship at all between social capital and tax fairness. (Nor is there a relationship between tax progressivity and racial diversity). Social capital's relationship to one indicator of welfare policy, maximum cash benefit levels, is significant prior to the mid-1990s. The disappearance of that effect once states were granted increased discretion on welfare eligibility is baffling, and it leads one to wonder about the implications that can be drawn about social capital and welfare policy.

Not unlike the evidence considered in the preceding chapters (especially Chapters 4 and 5), there is at best limited evidence to suggest that social capital is important for the issues (dependent variables) examined here. As with previous research (including that on political culture and relative social outcomes), social capital and political culture has little clear or consistent bearing on policy outputs – with a few possible exceptions. In general, however, there is not much evidence of a carryover or "transmission belt" effect from the civic to the public policy arenas. In contrast, it appears that race and diversity played a larger role in affecting civil rights policy and had (and continues to have) important implications for welfare policy. For the policy outputs examined here, racial diversity is more significant than social capital, although future research should be directed toward better understanding their interactions as well as the role of other dimensions of social differentiation such as gender and class.

7

Conclusions

I began this book by posing a battery of questions about the relationship of race and community – of racial diversity and social capital – in American politics, positing that the two are likely intertwined and/or in tension in extensive and complex ways. In broad terms the question was whether racial considerations, and racial minority populations, have substantially affected the sense of community in America. Furthermore, I set out to systematically assess these two interpretations, each traceable to philosophical traditions in American politics, in relationship to one another as evidenced in state politics particularly. The social capital thesis has argued that civic association and sense of community have been a dominant influence in American politics, with a variety of powerful beneficial effects (while acknowledging that social capital may occasionally have a "dark side"). Social capital studies have provided a theoretical basis and extensive empirical evidence on behalf of its claims (see especially Putnam 2000 and Chapter 3 herein). The contemporary racial diversity thesis focuses on firmly acknowledging and systematically incorporating elements of the anti-egalitarianism tradition into scholarly inquiries, thereby seeking to understand the historical and recent implications of that legacy.

Exploration of these two interpretations quickly led me to confront an important puzzle in American politics research that structured the later empirical analyses. Higher *racial diversity* is associated with lesser and *less equitable* political processes and public policy outcomes (even after accounting for a variety of other factors; Hero 1998), yet higher levels of *social capital* are associated with *"better"* processes and outcomes (Putnam 2000). These facts pose questions about possible interrelations and interactions between the two social forces: whether one set of theoretical claims proved more accurate and whether either interpretation took the other sufficiently into account. If conditions are indeed better in high social capital settings then *for whom* are they better? Are they better for all (i.e., for a majority in absolute terms) or for some more than others (i.e., relatively)? Questions also arise concerning which evaluative standards – absolute versus relative indicators – should be used when making such judgments and whether alternative standards make much difference in the overall conclusions. Furthermore, it is evident that the evaluative criteria applied and the indicators used to assess evidence are themselves associated with a particular analytical perspective.

Although they are compelling in themselves, an additional reason to address and juxtapose these two analytical perspectives is that each has claimed that its core thesis applies to and can explain a *broad range* of issues. The social capital thesis emphatically asserts a significant (positive) impact on an array of social outcomes, on civic engagement, and on economic and civic equality in American politics (Putnam 2000; cf. Elazar 1984). However, one of weaknesses of social capital research as an analytical endeavor is that it does not itself intellectually "bridge" toward – that is, adequately take sufficient account of – other research and analytical perspectives that could yield a fuller understanding (cf. Hero 1991).

The racial diversity thesis has applied and extended its arguments to a broader range of issues than have leading social capital studies, and it did so several years before the publication in 2000 of Putnam's *Bowling Alone* (see Hero and Tolbert 1996; Hero 1998; also see Hero 1992; Orr 1999; cf. Putnam 2000). Furthermore, studies with an explicit racial diversity focus also assessed its claims relative to a concept acknowledged to be similar to and that preceded the social capital thesis, "political culture" (cf. Putnam 2000; Elazar 1984); a major conclusion was that racial diversity often matters regarding relative social outcomes for minorities compared to whites, but political culture had little or no impact on those outcomes. Hence, the findings concerning social capital and relative social outcomes discussed earlier (see Chapter 4) are clearly presaged in prior research (Hero 1998). Other explanations of social outcomes, such as public opinion and ideology (Erikson et al. 1993) also seemed less able to explain relative outcomes than was racial diversity (Hero 1998; but see Hawes et al. 2006). The diversity research also examined questions concerning whether "mediating institutions" of politics (such as political parties and interest groups), formal governmental institutions (e.g., the structures and processes of state legislatures, courts, and governors), and local government institutions were influenced by racial diversity (Hero 1998); some but not all of the evidence was consistent with the diversity argument.

So, what are the broad conclusions to be drawn about the explanatory power of racial diversity and social capital? On the whole, it seems the two theoretical perspectives, and the empirical reality they seek to describe, are indeed interrelated to some degree and perhaps mutually constitutive. However, when the two are separated the former (racial diversity) is more powerful than the latter – especially in explaining relative conditions – and is equally able to explain aggregate outcomes and conditions. Considerable evidence indicates that "community" has indeed been racially contingent, and the evidence developed here suggests that community cannot be appropriately understood without reference to racial diversity in America. This is not surprising given that the concept of community implies both inclusion and exclusion (cf. Orr 1999) and that race has been a fundamental basis for inclusion and exclusion in American politics. Positive impacts of aggregate social capital on various social outcomes seem virtually nonexistent when examining relative conditions for minorities. That is, the ostensibly salutary benefits of social capital do not extend to minority populations. And even aggregate participation and public policies show relatively little influence from social capital.

As noted in Chapter 2, social capital arguments have eloquently stated: "Race is such a fundamental feature of American social history that nearly every other feature of our society is connected to it in some way" (Putnam 2000, p. 279); and "Race is the most important embodiment of the ethical crosscurrents that swirl around the rocks of social capital in contemporary America" (p. 361). The evidence presented here suggests those claims are even more accurate and compelling than they initially appear – but in a way and to a degree that fundamentally contradicts social capital claims. When race is appropriately incorporated into the analysis – as we do in this study – racial diversity's importance almost always clearly surpasses that of social capital itself and/or indicates that effects purported to derive from social capital are partly or mainly due to racial factors. If one considers relative outcomes (as does the diversity thesis) rather than aggregate overall outcomes, which submerge the relative situation of minorities (as do social capital studies), the impact of diversity becomes manifest – as does the realization that many social capital claims are functions of its implicit focus on outcomes for white populations and of conditions in homogeneous white states. However, even in the aggregate the impact of social capital is not always strong, especially after taking account of other factors, and this appears to be the case for various dimensions of politics. In general, racial diversity is still a significant part of the social and political structure in broad and systemic ways (Hero 1992, 1998; King and Smith 2005). I now review the more specific evidence that supports these broader conclusions.

REVIEW OF THE MAJOR FINDINGS

The preceding chapters delineated and then examined the two perspectives, juxtaposing them regarding a number of social and political dimensions: social outcomes, civic and social equality (Chapter 4), patterns of participation (Chapter 5), and policy outputs (Chapter 6). I began by indicating the rather strong inverse relationship between the social capital index and the measure of racial diversity. I then focused on assessing social outcomes, the consequences that have been the empirical corner-stone in support of the social capital argument. Initially, it was clearly demonstrated (in Chapter 4; also see Hawes et al. 2006) that, when considering several social outcomes, the black/white ratios (within states) are consistently no better and are some-times worse when there is higher social capital (in the aggre-gate). Although I explained why *ratios* (i.e., within-state group comparisons) are the certainly the most appropriate measures to examine, I also analyzed group *rates* (i.e., across states) on those social outcomes. Yet the findings when examining minority to minority rates did not alter the conclusion about social capital's irrelevance for explaining social outcomes that had been shown in the analysis of ratios. A principal finding of this analysis is that social outcomes look quite different when disaggregated by racial groups than when lumped together and considered in the aggregate, as social capital studies have typically done. The assertion that higher social capital leads to better outcomes results almost entirely from the situation of whites, an interest-ing and important finding; it is also notable that white social capital seems weaker in states where there are larger minority populations. But the consequences of higher aggregate social capital for minorities scarcely exist and in fact are sometimes negative. On the whole, the findings in the first section of Chap-ter 4 dramatically undercut the assertions about the positive con-sequences of social capital, once we examine the issue of better *for whom*. Instead those findings make a strong case for the racially limited relevance of aggregate social capital, which is of particular significance because racial diversity and aggregate social capital are inversely related to begin with.

Another section in Chapter 4 assessed two elements relevant to "civic equality": voter registration and voter turnout of whites and minorities relative to overall social capital. By and large there is, again, virtually no evidence in support of the social capital thesis when the data are disaggregated by racial groups. There is limited data suggesting that rates of registration and turnout for whites may be higher where there is higher social capital, but this largely seems to reaffirm that social capital's explanatory reach is racially confined (when it can be discerned at all). Thus, the civic equality that is alleged to stem from higher aggregate social capital does not really extend to include minority populations.

The inegalitarian tradition includes racial as well as economic inequality (Smith 1997), and the two may be interconnected. Social capital's association with "economic" equality – measured as per capita income and poverty rates – of minority groups provides a bit of support for the social capital thesis. Per capita income ratios for minorities vary little in relation to social capital, but minority poverty rates are slightly improved where there is higher social capital. However, as for the social capital thesis in general – and perhaps especially relevant in this instance – the direction of causation is unclear. Social capital studies often speak of "association" rather than causation per se. One can readily imagine that less poverty "explains" levels of social capital as much as the reverse, and the significance of the finding and how much it actually supports the social capital thesis is accordingly less clear.

Taken alone or together, the evidence in Chapter 4 seems to me devastatingly *un*supportive, even contradictory, of the social capital thesis. To the extent that consequences or *social outcomes* are the linchpin of the social capital argument, which they certainly appear to be, the evidence presented here severely undermines the claims and makes very clear that the thesis is limited in its ability to explain important questions of racial inequality (also see Hawes et al. 2006).

We revisited the issues of participation, examining the impact of racial diversity together with social capital's direct, indirect, and interactive effects on overall voter turnout within states in presidential and congressional elections. We demonstrated direct effects both of racial diversity and of social capital on voter turnout rates in the states. Probably more important were the indications of indirect and interactive (or conditional) effects of race and social capital. A direct effect of racial diversity on turnout is clearly evident and is comparable in both presidential and congressional elections. The effect of social capital is large in presidential elections but much smaller in midterm elections; this latter result is somewhat puzzling in that social capital might be expected to have more impact in lower- than in higher-profile elections. Also notable is the linear relationship between racial diversity and voter participation and the nonlinear effect of social capital on turnout: the impact of racial diversity increases continually whereas social capital's impact on aggregate turnout does not increase after a certain point.

Because states with more racial diversity have lower social capital and in turn reduced turnout rates, the relationship between social capital and voter turnout may thus be partially endogenous. The direct effect of social capital on voter turnout was slightly larger than that of racial diversity in presidential elections, but the positive effect of social capital on turnout also seems conditioned by racial diversity. In states with high racial diversity, the positive effects of social capital on turnout rates decrease by about half in presidential elections and almost disappear in midterm elections. It is not clear which factor has greater impact individually; it probably depends on such other things as which set of elections are examined. In general, the aggregate approach to examining political participation (as distinct from the analysis of civic equality in Chapter 4) indicates the importance of racial diversity *and* of social capital regarding aggregate voter turnout. When we considered the interaction of diversity and social capital, a powerful dampening effect of the former on the latter was shown.

Combining survey data with contextual data allowed us to explore other dimensions. We showed that state racial diversity has a direct effect on individual voter turnout; in states with high racial diversity, people are less apt to vote in presidential elections, even after we control for a host of individual and state contextual variables. Racial diversity is the most consistent variable of all the state-level factors regarding voting, and it is the only one that is significant in the two election years considered. People who live in states with high social capital were more likely to vote in 1996, but this was not the case in 2000 when racial diversity is also taken into account; that is, persons living in states with more social capital were not more likely to vote in the 2000 elections.

The impact of state racial diversity is stronger still when we look at forms of political participation other than voting. In two years (1996 and 2000), respondents from states with higher racial diversity were significantly less likely to participate in various political acts. The significant negative relationship with a participation index we created was evident even after we accounted for an array of individual and state contextual factors commonly associated with political participation. Furthermore, social capital was *not* a significant predictor on the index of political participation – in either of the years examined – when racial diversity is considered in the analysis. This is quite surprising and is inconsistent with the social capital argument: we would expect social capital to be more important than diversity for nonelectoral participation. The implication is that state racial diversity has a more significant and perhaps broader impact on political participation than does a state's score on the social capital index (Putnam 2000). The data provide, then, considerable evidence that state racial diversity is associated with political participation in America. However, other contextual factors – particularly social capital but also a number of others (e.g., socioeconomic influences such as income, education, and urbanization) are not. The impact of racial diversity, and the lack of impact of the other contextual variables, is noteworthy (cf. Verba et al. 1995).

After examining the forms of participation together as part of an index, we examined them separately. People in states with higher social capital were not more likely to participate in any of the seven activities considered. State social capital was not a significant predictor of these other forms of political participation, including "attending political rallies" and "working for a political party," which were parts of the participation index used in some social capital studies (Putnam 2000). On the other hand, individuals in states with high racial diversity were significantly less likely to participate in five of the seven political activities. Racial diversity is an important contextual predictor of these various forms of nonelectoral political participation; social capital is not. Taken as whole, the analysis in Chapter 5 indicates there is evidence of a positive effect of social capital on voting, although the degree is less than anticipated and social capital's effects are more conditioned by race than previous studies have acknowledged. Moreover, social capital has little to no impact on certain other forms of participation whereas racial diversity does. One suspects that social capital's effects may be relevant to the civic arena but rather less so to the political one (cf. Stone et al. 2001; Theiss-Morse and Hibbing 2005).

Social capital analyses have not usually considered policy *outputs* as distinct from social *outcomes*. But there are good reasons to consider policies given the assumption that we might (and perhaps should) expect some congruence between formal governmental actions and such purportedly significant forces in society as social capital and race. Yet social capital seems *not* to be related to important policies relevant to basic equality (e.g., states' civil rights policies prior to the federal legislation of the 1960s) and tax fairness, although racial diversity's impact on the former (but not the latter) seems clear; see Chapter 6. I acknowledge, however, that the evidentiary basis for our civil rights analysis is not as strong as I would wish.

There is some evidence of social capital's effect on welfare policy, but exactly what to make of it is not entirely obvious.

To begin with, the impact of social capital may not apply to all indicators or dimensions of welfare policy. And even though we showed social capital to be strongly related to one indicator of welfare policy – cash benefit levels – in the 1980s and early 1990s this impact vanishes following the major welfare reform legislation of 1996. This is a counterintuitive and confusing result, since one would expect the impact of social capital to be greater after the reform legislation, which gave states greater discretion than before; yet we find the reverse.

In assessing welfare policy it is also important to recall that the foundation or "baseline" of the American welfare state was racially constrained from the outset (see, e.g., Lieberman 2003). Hence, considerations of various social outcomes before and after the decline of social capital should bear this in mind. When one examines the contemporary welfare state, then, evidence of the racial effects that are found are in part an extension of the racial bias imbedded in the formative stages and evolution of welfare policy. Racial diversity has been shown to have shaped civil rights policies in the states (Dye 1969) and in turn to have influenced state welfare policy by formally including (or formally prohibiting the exclusion) of minorities on racial grounds, which had occurred prior to the mid-1960s (Albritton 1990). On the whole, the policy outputs we examined give ample support to the racial diversity perspective but little support for social capital claims.

In addition, the several findings on policy outputs in Chapter 6 broadly echo those of previous research. Recall that Knack's (2002) study, which arrived at conclusions that were generally supportive of the social capital thesis, nonetheless indicated that aspects of social capital identified with "social connectedness" tended not to be related to the dependent variable in his research (governmental performance), whereas aspects of social capital identified with "generalized reciprocity" were. Hill and Matsubayashi (2005) found that more "bridging" social capital is not related to more responsive government but that more "bonding" social capital is related to less responsive government.

Thus, other research seeking to test the social capital thesis has provided qualified support at best, and the support for core issue of connectedness (which is relevant to the bridging elements of community) have fared least well in these analyses of social capital's policy implications. The principel empirical findings of Chapters 4–6 are summarized in Table 7-1.

The implications of the empirical findings listed in Table 7-1 – along with the arguments made in preceding chapters and sections of the present chapter – suggest a set of general conclusions and comparisons. Figure 7-1 sketches out broad relationships between civil society, its inclusiveness or level of (racial) integration, and the degree of formal/political equality as implied in Putnam's *Bowling Alone* (*BA*) on the one hand and, on the other hand, as viewed through the lens of the racial diversity thesis as I have developed it. In a sense, this figure indicates the intersection of de facto *civic* relations and de jure *political* institutions. To be sure, the figure very much oversimplifies and hence is not able to capture all complexity and nuance, and others will question some of the characterizations and placements of concepts. However, the figure is intended to be more illustrative and suggestive than definitive.

It seems to me the overall portrayal in *BA* of American civil society and its relation to the formal dimension of political life (to the extent the latter is addressed; see Chapter 6) is quite positive and accordingly implies conditions toward the upper right quadrant of the figure. That is, there is the suggestion of high civic association and high political engagement, if not direct de jure procedural equality (see "Overall *Assertions* of *BA*/*SC*)." In contrast, my contention is that the *reality* of the era from the 1940s to about 1965 is more complicated. While there was high civic association and political equality for whites, there was also formal and informal racial segregation and a "sectarian" condition that varied in form and intensity across the country (cf. Putnam 2000, p. 355; the civil rights legislation of the mid-1960s, which coincided with the decline of social capital, modified this). Hence, more explicit recognition of the racial ordering leads to

TABLE 7-1. *Summary of Empirical Findings (Chapters 4–6)*

	Are findings supportive of social capital (SC) thesis as it relates to minorities?
Social outcomes[a]	
Graduation ratios	No (contradict the SC thesis)
(Graduation rates)	Yes
Suspension ratios	No (contradict the SC thesis)
(Suspension rates)	No
Incarceration ratios	No (contradict the SC thesis)
(Incarceration rates)	No
Infant mortality ratios	No
(Infant mortality rates)	No
Civic quality[a]	
Registration ratios	No (contradict the SC thesis)
(Registration rates)	No
Turnout ratios	No (contradict the SC thesis)
(Turnout rates)	No
Economic equality[a]	
Per capita income ratios	Yes (direction of causation?)
(Per capita income rates)	Maybe (direction of causation?)
Poverty ratios	No
(Poverty rates)	Maybe (direction of causation?)

Participation:

Both social capital and racial diversity have direct effects on voter turnout in presidential and congress ional elections (variation by elections; some effects are linear but others are not)

Indirect effects of diversity on social capital, and, in turn, on aggregate turnout

Substantial Interactive effects: racial diversity strongly dampens impacts of social capital on turnout

Other forms of participation (controlling for context)

Voting: impact of diversity, no impact of social capital

Index of participation: no impact of social capital; significant impact of diversity

Indicators from index of participation examined separately: no impact of social capital; significant impact of diversity

General conclusion: Racial diversity usually stronger than social capital as predictor of participation.

TABLE 7-1 *(continued)*

Policy Outputs	Are findings supportive of social capital (SC) thesis as it relates to minorities?	
	Support for social capital thesis?	Support for diversity thesis?
Civil Rights policies	No	Yes
Tax progressivity	No	No
Welfare	Unclear[b]	Yes

[a] For each of the three areas – social outcomes, civic equality, and economic equality – the *ratios* are minority rates to white rates within states. The *rates* that are noted in parentheses are the rates for racial/ethnic groups in one state compared to another (i.e., across states); they are listed in parentheses because they are arguably not the appropriate indicators to consider given the arguments of the two analytical perspectives. See also Hawes et al. (2006).

[b] Yes before reform but no after reform.

substantially different characterizations than those offered in *BA* (King and Smith 2005).

I suggest that partial political pluralism (Schatttschneider 1960; Stone 1980) and racially hierarchical or two-tiered pluralism (Pinderhughes 1987; Hero 1992; Dawson 2001) emerged after the civil rights era (and the decline of social capital); this is shown in the bottom right of the figure. This entails higher formal (and improved but hardly complete substantive) equality and also indicates a decline in social capital overall (as understood in social capital studies). However, as I have argued, a case could be made that there is now more social capital than before if one incorporates the greater egalitarianism of the political and civic arenas in the post-1960s period.

Viewed in these ways, both formal and informal dimensions associated with racial diversity and social capital are included as important elements of politics, but the two analytical perspectives differ on the degree of influence – and the particular implications – of the corresponding social forces in the American polity. Another point is suggested. It has been previously argued (Hero 1992) that the second (racialized) tier of "two-tiered

FIGURE 7-1. Assertions of Social Capital and the Reality of Racial Circumstances

Formal/Political Equality
(especially for Black/Minorities)

	Low	High
High		[Ideal]
	Civic association	*Full equality*
	(for whites, in *BA*)	*Strong community*
		(Overall *Assertions* of *BA*/SC)
		[before SC decline]
Informal/Civil Society's Inclusiveness– Integration (especially re blacks/minorities)	"Sectarian" (Blacks' *Reality* in *BA*) [before SC decline]	Partial political Pluralism
		Two-tiered Pluralism
	Most inequality/ Exclusion	
Low	[Worst case]	

(*BA = Bowling Alone*; SC = Social Capital)

pluralism" must and should be considered in relationship to the workings of the first tier (i.e., "standard pluralism") and vice versa; the discussion here similarly suggests that social capital or "community" interpretations should systematically incorporate racial diversity insights and vice versa (Smith 1993; Schneider and Ingram 1993). In terms of both empirical democratic theory and political practice, reconciling racial diversity and notions of community are major challenges for American democracy and for scholars of American politics. Additionally, unraveling the complexity of racial diversity, by better explaining interconnections of race and social class, poses another challenge (Hero and Radcliff 2005; Jacobs and Skocpol 2005). The role of mediating institutions that link civil society and formal political entities – that is, the actions of political parties and interest groups – will also need to be studied as part of the diversity–community nexus (Skocpol 2003; Frymer 2005; Wolbrecht 2005).

THE RELATIVE STATUS OF SOCIAL CAPITAL AND RACIAL DIVERSITY ARGUMENTS

The analysis in this book suggests that race and community – racial diversity and social capital – are interconnected phenomena in American politics. At the same time, juxtaposing the social capital and racial diversity theses casts serious doubt on the accuracy of the former and provides considerable support for the latter. Yet social capital and similar arguments remain popular and well received in both public discourse and scholarly research, as suggested by a large body of popular and academic writings, scholarly conferences focused on the theory, and the large amount of funding that supports research on social capital. How is it that social capital arguments receive such fervent continued acceptance and fervent support despite a substantial body of research that has not only challenged but has even strongly contradicted many of its claims, including some based on contrary findings related to racial diversity in America (see Hero 2003a, b, 1998). Why have the questions and vast contrary evidence had so little impact on the intellectual standing of social capital as a theoretical interpretation?

It is difficult to answer the question definitively, but I suggest some reasons that seem at least plausible. One reason is that social capital (if correct) seems able to explain a broad range of issues, as emphasized previously (see especially Chapter 2). That is, its ostensible breadth of empirical theoretical power and comprehensiveness is attractive. A second reason involves several related ideas.

The social capital thesis is appealing because it emphasizes and resonates with noble sentiments of community, consensus, and connectedness and hence is sociopsychologically comforting. Many *want* to believe it, and understandably so. It depicts potential social conditions and outcomes conducive to and consistent with the achievement of well-being, the pursuit of happiness, and "the good life" emerging from civic association. It provides a compelling (if arguably romanticized) version of

America's past and suggests a host of powerful and important salutary consequences of social capital. Although the socil capital thesis eloquently acknowledges the role of race in American history, *analytically* it is an essentially color-blind approach – that is, the impact of race is viewed as an unfortunate aberration that does not directly affect the basic understanding or measurement of important variables. This leads to shortcomings and problematic implications of the theory. Nor does this analytically color-blind approach detract from most of the larger claims that are put forth about social capital's benefits, at least as those are presented in the empirical evidence. Such an orientation comports well with the opinion, particularly prevalent among whites, that racial inequality has largely been addressed perhaps even solved as a result of civil rights and various related policies (cf. Hochschild 1995), and it is consistent with a pattern identified by Smith (1993) that scholarship in the civic republican traditions tends to slight the importance of race in American politics. This orientation is also not necessarily at odds with scholarship which, while admitting to considerable racial inequality, firmly suggests that economic inequality is more prominent and important than racial inequality in America (cf. Jacobs and Skocpol 2005).

What some scholars have asserted about the influence of the "political culture" thesis, a conceptual predecessor and cousin to social capital, also seems pertinent to explaining social capital's popularity. It has been said that "Elazar's cultural theory has *intuitive appeal* as it is *consistent with general impressions* about state differences in political values, style, and tone. It also provides a historical explanation for differences" (Gray 2004, p. 23; cf. Gray 1999, p. 24 emphases added). And considerable support has been found for the political culture argument (see, e.g., Fitzpatrick and Hero 1988, among many others), though the argument has also been strongly questioned (Thompson et al. 1990; Hero 1998).

It may well be that political culture (and/or social capital) interpretations have "intuitive appeal" to and are "consistent with [the] general impressions" of many. But those intuitions and impressions are not necessarily shared by all scholars and, more importantly, they do not stand up well when analyzed with extensive and appropriate evidence – particularly, evidence grounded in the racial diversity thesis. There is the old adage that "if something sounds too good to be true, it probably is." This adage certainly seems applicable to the social capital thesis, which (as the evidence in this book shows) explains dramatically less than has been previously argued and may be fundamentally wrong when it comes to issues of racial equality; by extension, the argument's normative appeal is presumably much diminished. One result of the uncritical acceptance of social capital claims it that we may mistake a problem for a solution. But other theories and associated contrary evidence have apparently had only a modest impact on the status of the social capital thesis as applied to the United States.

That racial inequality and high social capital coexisted from World War II until the mid-1960s is both telling and ironic. And that states with the highest levels of social capital are unusual in having low racial diversity, small population, low urbanization, and slow growth rates makes one wary of the argument in principle and leads to serious reservations about its theoretical validity and normative implications. These points seem to have escaped the attention of much social capital and related research as well as public intellectual discourse, however.

In some discussions of racial diversity and political culture it has been claimed that the racial diversity argument "need[s] to be confirmed and extended by other researchers before [it] will replace political subcultures as an explanation" (Gray 2004, p. 24; cf. Gray 1999, p. 26). However, a sizeable body of research has examined the racial diversity thesis in direct juxtaposition to political culture and found that, in virtually every instance, the impact of political culture is minimal or nonevident when diversity is also examined (Hero 1998; see Chapter 3 herein). Similarly, as demonstrated in the preceding chapters, social capital's impact is vastly diminished when considered along with racial diversity; this has been reaffirmed in other research (see Hawes et al. 2006). And a great deal of other evidence indicates the importance of race in American politics.

The point is *not* that racial diversity can explain all (or even most) of the most important issues in American state politics. However, the evidence in this study makes clear that social capital is often contradicted – and is much less well supported and persuasive – than it has generally been made out to be, and it certainly seems a weaker explanation of an important array of political issues than is racial diversity. Studies of racial diversity have been no less comprehensive than social capital (and political culture) studies, have provided at least as much evidence in support of their arguments, and have considered more alternative interpretations; nonetheless, they have been downplayed (Gray 1999). In short, social capital (and political culture) interpretations have held a privileged status among a substantial number of scholars compared to other arguments, a status that the evidence presented here suggests is not warranted. That social capital and political culture (especially the latter) have generally been inattentive to and have not fully incorporated racial diversity into their analyses is likewise notable. It is not clear exactly what we should make of this, but it does not seem entirely accidental.

RESEARCH AGENDAS

Now that we have compared theses, it may be useful to suggest some ideas for future research. The social capital argument (as presented by Putnam) does not spend a great deal of time seeking to explain the origins of social capital, since it is mostly concerned with documenting its decline and its consequences; Putnam (2000 pp. 292–4) does cite other works (Elazar 1984; Rice and Feldman 1997) that explore those origins. Few studies delve into the roots of social capital, but it is said that the patterns have "deep historical roots" and that there is a "striking . . . spatial correlation between low social capital at the end of the twentieth century and slavery in the first half of the nineteenth century"; moreover, "well-trod paths of immigration helped establish regional and local patterns of social capital in contemporary America." Thus there is a strong implication that the origins of social capital have significant racial/ethnic elements (Putnam 2000; cf. Elazar 1984). One wishes these issues were further pursued in social capital studies, because the unique traits of states where social capital is highest suggest the need for more exploration along these lines. Because immigration and related factors are leading to increased diversity, further elaboration of the roots of social capital might bring greater understanding of these important trends and how various social capital contexts might be expected to shape or be affected by those trends.

With further regard to roots or origins, social capital theorists have said little about the role of formal governmental institutions in shaping and/or reinforcing civic relationships and (presumably) social capital. The very formation and "rights" of state governments – and who was to count, and how much, for purposes of representation in Congress – was, of course, a major issue in the writing of the U.S. Constitution. The creation of counties, cities, school district boundaries, "neighborhood" school boundaries (within school districts), special districts, restrictive covenants, and legislative districts play some role in defining not only political jurisdictions but also social boundaries that affect social interactions (Burns 1994; Jones-Correa 2000). Battles over bussing – shaped by the boundaries of school districts, school attendance zones, racial segregation, and other factors – and a host of such controversies are in some part affected by the intersection of race and a sense of community (social capital), as captured in such phrases as "community control" and "neighborhood schools." One wonders whether decisions about jurisdictional boundaries and authority and their associated controversies should be thought of as causes or rather as consequences of social capital's racial dimensions (or as both). Furthermore, research has demonstrated the impact of electoral institutions and procedures on political behavior, like voting (Barreto, Segura, and Woods 2004). In addition to formal participation, we might anticipate that such institutions and policies would have consequences for other dimensions of civic engagement.

Some specific examples of a similar nature can be mentioned. For instance, the larger urban "reform" movement of the early 1900s profoundly affected the institutions and, in turn, the politics and policies of urban governments. Reform efforts were often advocated by "good government" groups and were typically rooted in arguments for broad, community, "public regarding" orientations. Good government groups, neighborhood improvement associations, and other positively labeled civic groups exemplify a supposedly "bridging" orientation, as assumed in social capital studies. That *may* be correct, but it is hardly indisputable. Research has shown that the reforms advanced – particularly at-large and nonpartisan elections – had important biases in favor of middle-class and against working-class voters as well as a bias toward Anglo versus ethnic populations. Scholars have also shown how the "slating" practices of good government groups in southwestern cities often made it difficult to elect minorities. Reform practices were especially dominant in the South and Southwest through much of the 1900s; it was not until the 1960s that reform institutions really came to be questioned, spurred by concerns over civil rights and questions of equal descriptive and substantive representation.

Explanations for the decline of social capital that have been offered thus far still seem unsatisfactory. One may accept that generational replacement along with other factors (television, urban sprawl, etc.) played a major role (see Putnam 2000, ch. 15), but it appears there must be more to the story. Also, given the importance attached to racial/ethnic and migration patterns in the *formation* of social capital (to the extent it is discussed; see Putnam 2000, pp. 292–4), it is not clear why such factors are not extensively examined as part of the explanation for the *decline* of social capital. That is, if the creation and levels of social capital are attributable (at least in part) to racial or ethnic influences then should we not expect that the decline of social capital was also affected by such influences?

It is hard to imagine that all of the familiar political and social developments of the 1960s did not affect broad social relationships and social capital patterns. Indeed, the express purpose of much of the legislation could be interpreted as seeking to break down existing unequal formal and informal social arrangements (Schattschneider 1960). It's quite possible, of course, that these policy developments had less impact in areas where the principal affected populations (i.e., minorities) were largely absent as in the most homogeneous contexts, which may explain why North Dakota and South Dakota are identified as having the highest levels of social capital.

As emphasized previously, civil rights policies were intended to achieve "simple justice"; in so doing, legislation and court decisions often overturned a host of exclusionary practices that had existed for decades that spanned the periods when social capital was said to be at its highest. Urban social change leading to increased racial representational equality was also fostered by the U.S. Supreme Court's "reapportionment revolution," which likewise disrupted long-standing arrangements (in effect during periods when social capital was said to be high) and which had resulted in malapportionment (Hill 1994). Indeed, it seems that the greatest advances in American racial equality have occurred precisely when traditional notions of community (dense social capital) were questioned, not lauded (Klinkner and Smith 1999).

This discussion of the civil rights era leads to another, arresting point: If we assume that the argument is correct with regard to the timing of social capital's decline – that it began in the mid-1960s (Putnam 2000) – then the United States has *never* experienced widespread high social capital (or a strong sense of "community") *and* high racial equality at the same time. If this is so, then we should think carefully about the relationship between racial inequality and community in America and consider whether the former has been an evil twin of the latter, whether they have indeed been the yin and yang as mentioned early in this book. It seems to me that this should also lead one to especially question the social capital argument itself. Is it somehow necessary that one but not the other – say, strong sense of community but not racial equality – can exist at one time, or has this simply been a historical reality in America but one that is not inevitable in principle? I leave that question for another day.

THEORETICAL INCLINATIONS

All theories are partial, of course. They are partial in the sense that they likely explain only a part of social phenomena and also in the sense that that they are predisposed to emphasize some ideas more than others. At issue, then, is what might be gained (or lost) by the specific partiality – the incompleteness and the analytical predisposition – of an individual theory. Even if one thinks that social capital's dispositions are correct, it is still useful to identify them. I have shown that the social capital thesis does not explain some of the core issues (i.e., social outcomes) that have been touted as a primary basis for its influence and thus that it is accurate to only a limited extent. The theory's adequacy is similarly in question because it leaves other factors insufficiently explored and neither acknowledges nor addresses a number of problematic social practices that flourished during the height of social capital and are inconsistent with the theory's claims about equality. Social capital arguments tend – consciously or not – to concern the circumstances of whites and not of minorities; this is indicated by its focus on (a) absolute rather than relative indicators of social well-being and (b) social outcomes rather than policy outputs. In sum, the importance of race and social change is systematically understudied.

Social capital studies also emphasize social cooperation rather than social and political competition. They are oriented toward consensus rather than conflict as a social process, to commonality rather than differences, to civic engagement more so than political involvement; social capital theories also seem to normatively privilege those values listed first over those listed second. One may well agree that inclinations in behalf of community organizational life, volunteering for civic activities, informal sociability, and so on are prima facie desirable activities. But their positive qualities are not necessarily transmitted to the public sphere. Indeed, it has been suggested that *civic* association and engagement may be associated with a desire to avoid difficult, messy, and contentious *political* questions via the alternative of involvement in informal and more congenial voluntary activities (Theiss-Morse and Hibbing 2005).

We can describe additional implications of social capital's relative inattention to race. In touting the virtues of its core concepts and in its way of measuring them, the social capital thesis mistakes numerical (white) *majority* relations for "the whole," essentially submerging the situation of minorities within the racially homogeneous (white) contexts – as in the Dakotas, Vermont, and virtually all other states that score high on the "social capital index." Although social capital and racial diversity correlate and overlap to some degree, when both are considered the impact of race consistently trumps that of social capital. The impact of race is deeper, wider, more pervasive, and more profound. Social capital studies miss this in overlooking how conditions for minorities differ from those for the majority and hence the possible existence of what some have called "racial apartheid" (Massey and Denton 1993) or of a racially two-tiered political system (Hero 1992; Orr 1999). This also occurs in part because "helping one's own" and "helping others" – bonding versus bridging – may be more or less likely in different racial contexts, something that is not captured in most existing social capital data and analysis. One consequence of its analytical orientation is that the effects of social capital are rather more apparent than real; much of its positive impact and ostensibly general social relevance fades when racial diversity is systematically brought into the picture.

AN OPTIMISTIC NOTE ON DIVERSITY AND SOCIAL CAPITAL

It is possible that conclusions about America's declining levels of social capital, so disconcerting to social capital theorists and many others, would be less disturbing if thought about considered and hence measured differently – through an inclusive, racial diversity lens. Assertions about the decline of social capital were based in part on survey responses to questions where dramatic decreases in civic engagement and other aspects of "civicness" were shown. Based on its theoretical premises and orientation, that is surely relevant evidence for social capital research. However, if social capital is conceived of and measured differently – that is, by asking different questions – then different inferences might be drawn. For example, imagine if questions were posed in the post–civil rights era (the aftermath of social capital's decline) regarding whether respondents have been "engaged in *racially integrated* civic associations or organizations" (rather than merely "engaged in civic associations or organizations"), have "attended meetings at *racially desegregated* school," "participated in procedurally *racially inclusive* elections," "been able to seek living quarters *under "'fair housing' conditions*," and so on. Posed thusly, we would almost certainly find that the level of social capital *increased* after the mid-1960s, and significantly so (although major issues of racial inequality remain, as we have shown). Asking questions in these ways – acknowledging the formal racial equality that has occurred – raises distinct possibilities that answers would not only indicate more social capital but also be more in the spirit of normatively desirable "bridging" social capital (as emphasized by Putnam 2000).

It is also possible that Putnam's social capital findings captured a unique period of adjustment or transition in American civil society as it adapted to the civil rights era and its aftermath. If so, and if we eventually see a more civic era begin to emerge (though it may not be civic in the same way the pre-1960s were), then this new era would be one more firmly rooted in egalitarian premises. A recent study that created an updated, "dynamic" social capital measure that parallels and correlates strongly with Putnam's measure of social capital suggests that "aggregate data indicate that social capital began to rise after 1995" but did not reach its pre-1990s level (Hawes et al. 2006, p.17). There may thus be some signs, if only tentative, of a resuscitation of social capital. Perhaps, paradoxically, the several comments I have offered here sound like "romantic" arguments (cf. Hero 1991). In any case, the interrelationships of race and social capital should be studied further and more carefully in the future.

What are the shortcomings of the diversity thesis? There are several. The concept and the measure of diversity are rather blunt analytical instruments. What is meant and entailed by diversity and what the tallying of racial configurations really means is not entirely self-evident, because the numbers obscure a great deal of social complexity. As noted at the outset, the size of minority populations seems somehow to capture or serve as surrogate for a broad array of interconnected contemporary social and political relationships that are the legacy of complicated histories. The true level of complexity is surely much greater than implied by the indicators used here. For example, in some instances our measure of diversity simply combined (say) the black and Latino percentages of the popultion; in other research diversity has been measured in different ways. However, two states with similar overall levels of diversity could differ in important ways. For instance, some states (e.g., Mississippi and South Carolina) have a minority population consisting almost entirely of blacks, whereas states with a similar overall level of diversity may (like New Mexico) have minority populations that are almost entirely Hispanic. This raises various questions, including the relationships *between* minority groups and even within minority groups, which has not explored here but has begun to be a topic of research. These caveats are just the tip of the iceberg, and one could readily identify variations on the themes noted. Diffrent configurations of minority and white populations would likely produce different politics and civic associational patterns. Also, diversity has been further complicated by the sizable immigration of recent decades.

Although racial diversity shows a significant relationship to numerous social outcomes, participation patterns, and policy dimensions, the specific causal mechanism is not entirely clear.

The finding that diversity is negatively related to aggregate outcomes yet positively associated with relative outcomes suggests a "threshold" effect and a nonlinear relationship, where "racial threat" (as perceived by whites) may eventually translate into a level of minority political clout that can lessen (if not banish) inequality (cf. Fording 2001; Hero 1998, p. 144; Keiser et al. 2004). I suspect that the aggregate negative relationship is the result of attitudes and beliefs within and across groups as well as of informal and formal political institutions, social norms and practices, economic relations, religious dispositions, and a host of other factors. Attitudes and beliefs may in turn stem from "old fashioned" racism, "symbolic" racism, (perceived) group "threat," or "social dominance" (see the discussion that follows); and the relative importance of each of these views may vary by context – that is, as the size of racial minority populations is larger or smaller. But a mere listing of potentially relevant factors ultimately begs the questions of interest: How, how much, and under what (specific) circumstances do certain social and political experiences occur with implications that are relevant to racial outcomes? The answers are neither simple nor obvious.

One of the most direct accounts of the negative relationships attributes unequal outcomes for minorities to (a) the biases and assumptions embedded in the standard operating procedures of governmental agencies, which often do not uniformly treat people in different situations, (b) the electoral practices of local governments, especially regarding district versus at-large elections, and (c) differences in race, economic status, and similar factors that often reinforce the inequalities apparent in civil society. Nonetheless, how institutions reinforce, exacerbate, or undercut racial diversity needs to be much better articulated in diversity research. Case studies as well as extensive historical and institutional analyses should be part of the research approaches toward this goal. Government may not only reflect popular sentiments; indeed it may also have certain independent proclivities. We can expect the sentiments and proclivities of government to be more consistent with those of dominant group members than of minorities. Governments "respond" to majority group preferences and "react" to those of racial minorities (Johnson 2003). The literature on the "social construction" of target groups (Schneider and Ingram 1993) makes similar arguments. This suggests that the cumulative effect of individual attitudes is part of what explains racial diversity's negative impacts. On the other hand, the positive association of levels of diversity on relative indicators suggests some ability to dampen the extent of inequality; governments' reactions may be modulated by racial context. Although there is evidence of a dampening effect on inequality as a function of the size of the minority population, equality has seldom, in fact, been achieved.

Some would suggest that the biases associated with the diversity thesis are the obverse those associated with social capital arguments. That is, it could be said that diversity arguments may emphasize difference rather than commonality, the political situation of racial minorities more so than whites, competition rather than cooperation, conflict rather than consensus as social processes, relative versus absolute indicators, and inequality rather than equality. There may be some truth to that, but in many ways this is the very point of racial diversity arguments. In other words, the dimensions emphasized in diversity studies are precisely those that are neglected in many studies of American politics, and social capital studies are a leading example of such oversight. A fuller and more accurate understanding of American politics requires just such emphases, as the evidence presented in this study makes plain. The "other" side of American politics is no less significant than that emphasized in social capital and other studies. Furthermore, criticisms that may follow from alleged biases of the diversity argument should recognize that most diversity studies do at least consider – and often extensively examine – alternative arguments, including those offered by social capital, political culture, and socioeconomic theorists (cf. Hero 1998, 2003a,b).

RACE VERSUS PRINCIPLES: PARALLELS
IN OTHER RESEARCH

The general focus of this book has been on two broad, macro-level perspectives. However, it may also speak indirectly to and be informed by a body of individual-level (survey and experimentally based) literature on race and politics in America. The debates and differences between the macro-level theories of diversity and social capital seem to parallel certain debates of political psychologists who study race at the micro level in seeking to explain attitudes about such "race-based" policies as affirmative action.

One school of thought on individual attitudes toward multi-cultural policies claims that widely shared values, principles, and (cultural) orientations that are core elements of the "American Creed" – including fundamental fairness, equality, and individualism – are the critical explanation of those attitudes. Race is said to have become largely inconsequential in affecting attitudes about racially targeted policies. On the other hand, several other perspectives challenge, in part or in whole, the argument that principles and not race affect these attitudes. These latter perspectives contend that beliefs and attitudes about racially focused public policies are explained by (a) racial resentment, (b) racial group interests and competition, and/or (c) desires on the part of dominant groups in society to maintain and perhaps advance their group's status and privilege. Such explanations imply the importance of *anti*-egalitarian views that emerge from various sentiments. The argument that claims principles matter most is like the social capital thesis in implying that *general* social orientations are critical and that race is not essential or its impact has receded. The "racial resentment" explanation straddles the principled and the anti-egalitarian themes, and explanations (b) and (c) emphasize race and diversity most directly.

The argument of "principles," advanced most prominently by Sniderman, Crosby, and Hawell (2000), is that opposition to affirmative action policies is based on political values. That is, attitudes about those policies are rooted in beliefs about basic fairness and procedural egalitarianism – without race as a defining element – as core components of contemporary values. According to this view, it is the dislike of the policies per se, not the ethnic or other traits of the policies' beneficiaries that are pivotal. Affirmative action or other (racially) redistributive policy is opposed because it is viewed as violating fundamental principles. This leads to expectations that conservative ideology is associated with less support for (or more opposition to) racial policies, but the racial traits of program recipients are purportedly not the real issue (Sniderman et al. 2000; cf. Gilens 2003).

The three other perspectives – explanations (a), (b), and (c) – all challenge the principled politics argument in various ways and to various degrees. The *racial resentment* view contends that while old-fashioned racism has subsided in American society, negative attitudes toward blacks (and other minorities) are now expressed in symbolic ways. That is, although whites generally do not express directly hostile views, they nonetheless believe that the attitudes and behaviors of minorities are not consistent with mainstream American values. Hence white resentment of minorities and of policies seen as disproportionately benefiting minorities is based on perceptions (arguably stereotypes) concerning an alleged lack of "work ethic," "self-reliance," "impulse control," and "respect for authority" (Sears et al. 2000, p. 17).

Another view is that whites oppose racially oriented policies because they perceive minorities "as a competitive threat for valued social resources, status, and privileges." This *group competition* view contends there are real material interests at stake in the debate regarding policies targeted at minorities when those policies go beyond having solely a nondiscriminatory intent (Bobo 2000, pp. 142–3). Those conflicting interests lead to negative intergroup attitudes. Finally, *social dominance* "asserts that one's commitment to equality is likely to be related to the social status of one's group, with members of dominant groups being more resistant to the redistribution of resources and less likely to endorse principles of equality" (Sidanius et al. 2000, p. 196). An individual's social dominance orientation is what largely explains and leads to their holding certain political values – particularly anti-egalitarian views – which in turn are "behind the resistance to redistributive policies, such as affirmative action, especially among dominants." That is, the argument of the social dominance school is that values and principles are *themselves* racially shaped and racially contingent. In that regard this analytical perspective – along with the group competition and, to a lesser degree, the racial resentment arguments – have something in common with the racial diversity thesis, which implies that attitudes, including those about "community" and its inclusiveness or exclusiveness, are themselves racially conditioned. The social dominance and group competition views claim, essentially, that "principles" are endogenous; I have suggested in the previous chapters that a roughly similar relationship exists between racial diversity and social capital.

The issues examined in this book have not, to be sure, been about racially targeted policies or affirmative action. But the broad egalitarian values and salutary beneficial effects attributed to high social capital and to American principles seem not to extend to racial minorities with regard to an array of social outcomes and policy outputs or to civic and political equality, generally. Where white majority populations are large (in homogeneous settings), those principles and values are more readily attained overall; but the relative conditions for minorities are not necessarily better even here. (In homogeneous settings the relatively poor outcomes for the small minorities may stem as much from symbolic racism as from the other micro-level views noted.) Where minority populations are larger, the occurrence of racial resentment – as well as beliefs about racial competition and attitudes about social dominance among whites – are heightened and, through collective weight and collective effect, lead to patterns of inequality associated with racial hierarchy. This need not be entirely conscious, because the numbers and relative social status of whites compared to minorities is sufficiently overwhelming that it "just happens." Minority political mobilization may mitigate the degree of relative inequality but does not remove it entirely.

To the extent that our analysis of social capital and diversity has paralleled the "principles" versus "dominance" interpretations (respectively) in research on political psychology, there is more evidence for racial diversity and dominance arguments than for those of social capital and principles. Equality and community are highly valued, but these are too often abstracted from the broader (racial) context in the approaches of social capital and principled politics, as they have also been in political culture analyses (cf. Hero 1998). To some degree those interpretations seem to be romanticized. A more realistic view is one that acknowledges the differentiation and inequality demonstrated by the theory and evidence of the macro-level social diversity argument and of the micro-oriented racial resentment, group competition, and social dominance perspectives.

Racial attitudes may be affected not only by the size but also by the spatial dispersion of groups. This may help explain the impact of diversity as well as the patterns of civic association and whether those patterns are more bridging or bonding in nature. Recent research suggests that negative attitudes toward minority groups are shaped by the degree of group segregation and by the sheer size of the group. Negative attitudes among whites toward minority groups are strongest as the minority group is larger *and* more residentially segregated (Rocha 2006). Such evidence should be acknowledged and appropriately incorporated into future racial diversity and social capital research.

RACIAL DIVERSITY AND KINDRED AMERICAN POLITICS RESEARCH ORIENTATIONS

As we have noted a number of times, social capital arguments emphasize beneficial consequences of consensus, cooperation, and community for the well-being of American society. But there are other traditions in American politics and in political science research that approach American democracy somewhat differently. The diversity perspective has revealed that community has not necessarily been compatible with racial equality. And other scholars have argued that the advance of racial equality in the United States has occurred primarily under the unique circumstances when social quietude has been disrupted (Klinkner and Smith 1999) – when the legacy of racial inequality is joined with minority mobilization and other forces that lead to a challenge of prevailing norms. Perhaps it would be useful to close with some thoughts from an eminent political scientist who argued – on the eve of the civil rights movement and just before the decline of social capital – for another interpretation that parallels (and is consistent with) the racial diversity perspective on American politics.

In a seminal work, *The Semisovereign People: A Realist's View of Democracy*, E. E. Schattschneider (1960) argued that differences, competition, and even conflict are essential elements of politics and are certainly more essential than social quiescence. "[T]he central political fact in a free society is the tremendous contagiousness of conflict." The outcome of all conflict is, according to Schattschneider, "determined by the *scope* of its contagion" (1960, p. 2, emphasis in original), that is, by how widely – across groups, space, and governmental jurisdictions – political conflict and involvement take place.

"A look at political literature shows there has ... been a long-standing struggle between conflicting tendencies toward the privatization and socialization of conflict. ... A tremendous amount of conflict is controlled by keeping it so private that it is almost completely invisible." Here Schattschneider emphasizes ideas such as individualism and private enterprise, rather than "community," as sources of privatizing conflict. But one of the themes of our study is that community has not necessarily encouraged social connectedness (cf. Stone et al. 2001; Knack 2002; Theiss-Morse and Hibbing 2005) and may actually constrain it, in part because (i) the concept of community implies that some are insiders while others are outsiders and (ii) a frequent basis for the insider – outsider distinction in the United States has often been race. Furthermore, social capital studies have strongly implied the desirability of addressing social issues through the civic rather than the political arena (Putnam 2000; see also Chapter 6 herein). Theiss-Morse and Hibbing (2005) have argued, in ways entirely consistent with the spirit of Schattschneider's assertions, that civic associations and patterns of volunteering commonly have the effect of constraining the scope, extent, and nature of issues addressed in the political rather than the civic arena. These authors (and others) also contend that individuals are drawn to civic associations whose members are people "like me" (like oneself) and that people often join associations because they wish to be involved in a way that avoids conflict and "hard" questions.

Schattschneider (1960, p. 7) adds that it is "easy to identify another battery of ideas contributing to the socialization of conflict": "Ideas concerning equality, consistency, equal protection of the laws, justice... and civil rights tend to socialize conflict." He goes on to argue that "[t]he nationalization of politics inevitably breaks up old local power monopolies and old sectional power complexes; as a matter of fact, the new dimension produces so great a change in the scale of organization and the locus of power that it may take on a semirevolutionary character" (p. 11).

The point here is that Schattschneider, writing only a few years before the adoption of major civil rights legislation, recognized the tension between competing ideas in American politics. And he argued that concerns about equality and justice usually require the expansion of conflict – something well beyond social capital's "bridging" – and that breaking up certain established social relations are essential to fostering egalitarian goals. To the extent that Schattschneider's claim is true, it increases the plausibility of a stronger than coincidental connection between the rise of civil rights and the decline of social capital. Furthermore, that racial diversity continues to be significantly and negatively associated with (relative) social outcomes, civic and economic inequality, and policy outputs suggests that those established social relations have a legacy that is more telling than the salutary benefits of community that are highlighted in social capital studies.

The evidence in this book underscores that community in America has been and continues to be racially delimited. However much one wishes this were not the case, the evidence strongly suggests that it is. One might wish that high social capital entails racially and economically equitable distributions of salutary outcomes in America, but the evidence simply does not support that view. From a normative standpoint, I certainly wish it did. For some time America's sense of community has been racially contingent, or so a realistic analysis and understanding of American politics strongly suggests. More fully grasping how and why race continues to have so much impact is a major task for those concerned about American politics, especially those who systematically seek to understand it.

References

Abramson, Paul R. 1983. *Political Attitudes in America*. San Francisco: Freeman.

Albritton, Robert. 1990. "Social Services: Welfare and Health," in Virginia Gray, Herbert Jacob, and Robert B. Albritton (Eds.), *Politics in the American States*, 5th ed. Glenview, IL: Scott, Foresman, pp. 411–16.

Barreto, Matthew, Gary M. Segura, and Nathan Woods. 2004. "The Mobilizing Effect of Majority–Minority Districts on Latino Turnout," *American Political Science Review* 98, 1: 65–76.

Beck, Nathaniel, and Jonathan Katz. 1995. "What to Do (and Not to Do) with Time Series – Cross-Section Data," *American Political Science Review* 89, 4: 634–47.

Bernstein, Robert, Anita Chadha, and Robert Montjoy. 2001. "Overreporting Voting: Why It Happens and Why It Matters," *Public Opinion Quarterly* 65, 1: 22–44.

Bernstein, Robert, Anita Chadha, and Robert Montjoy. 2004. "Cross-State Bias in Voting and Registration Overreporting in Current Population Surveys," *State Politics and Policy Quarterly* 3, 4: 367–86.

Bimber, Bruce A. 2003. *Information and American Democracy: Technology in the Evolution of Political Power*. Cambridge University Press.

Bobo, Lawrence. 2000. "Race and Beliefs about Affirmative Action," in David O. Sears, Jim Sidanius, and Lawrence Bobo (Eds.), *Racialized Politics: The Debate About Racism in America*. University of Chicago Press, pp. 137–64.

Bowler, Shaun, Todd Donovan, and Eric D. Lawrence. 2005. "Choosing Democracy: On the Creation of Initiative Institutions in the American States," Paper presented at the Annual Meeting of the American Political Science Association, Washington, DC.

Brehm, John, and Wendy Rahn. 1997. "Individual-Level Evidence for the Causes and Consequences of Social Capital," *American Journal of Political Science* 41, 4: 999–1023.

Brown, Robert. 1995. "Party Cleavages and Welfare Effort in the American States," *American Political Science Review* 89, 1: 23–33.

Burns, Nancy. 1994. *The Formation of American Local Governments: Private Values in Public Institutions.* New York: Oxford University Press.

Campbell, Angus, Philip E. Converse, Warren E. Miller, and Donald E. Stokes. 1960. *The American Voter.* University of Chicago Press.

Carmines, Edward G., and James A. Stimson. 1989. *Issue Evolution: Race and the Transformation of American Politics.* Princeton, NJ: Princeton University Press.

Clarke, Susan E., Rodney E. Hero, Mara Sidney, Luis R. Fraga, and Bari A. Erlichson. 2006. *Multiethnic Moments: The Politics of Urban Education Reform.* Philadelphia: Temple University Press.

Conway, Margaret. 1991. *Political Participation in the United States*, 2nd ed. Washington, DC: Congressional Quarterly Press.

Crawford, Susan, and Peggy Levitt. 1999. "Social Change and Civic Engagement: The Case of the PTA," in Theda Skocpol and Morris P. Fiorina (Eds.), *Civic Engagement in American Democracy.* Washington, DC: Brookings, pp. 249–96.

Crowley, Jocelyn Elise, and Theda Skocpol. 2001. "The Rush to Organize: Explaining Associational Formation in the United States, 1860s to 1920s," *American Journal of Political Science* 45, 4: 813–29.

Dahl, Robert A. 1996. "Equality versus Inequality," *PS: Political Science* 29, 4: 462–7.

Dawson, Michael C. 2001. *Black Visions: The Roots of Contemporary African-American Political Ideologies* Chicago: University of Chicago Press.

DuBois, W. E. B. 1935. *Black Reconstruction.* New York: Harcourt, Brace.

Dye, Thomas R. 1969. "Inequality and Civil Rights Policy in the States," *Journal of Politics* 31, 4: 1080–97.

Dye, Thomas R. 1984. "Party and Policy in the States," *Journal of Politics* 46, 4: 1097–1116.

Elazar, Daniel J. 1966. *American Federalism: A View from the States.* New York: Crowell.

Elazar, Daniel J. 1972. *American Federalism: A View from the States*, 2nd ed. New York: Crowell.

Elazar, Daniel J. 1984. *American Federalism: A View from the States*, 3rd ed. New York: Harper & Row.

Erikson, Robert S., Gerald C. Wright, and John P. McIver. 1993. *Statehouse Democracy: Public Opinion and Policy in the United States.* Cambridge University Press.

Feldman, Stanley, and Marco R. Steenbergen. 2001. "The Humanitarian Foundation of Public Support for Social Welfare," *American Journal of Political Science* 45, 3: 658–77.

Fellowes, Matthew C., and Gretchen Rowe. 2004. "Politics and the New American Welfare State," *American Journal of Political Science* 48, 2: 362–73.

Fishman, Robert M. 2004. *Democracy's Voices: Social Ties and the Quality of Public Life in Spain*. Ithaca, NY: Cornell University Press.

Fitzpatrick, Jody L., and Rodney E. Hero. 1988. "Political Culture and Political Characteristics of the American States: A Consideration of Some Old and New Questions," *Western Political Quarterly* 41, 1: 145–53.

Fording, Richard C. 2001. "The Political Response to Black Insurgency: A Test of Competing Images of the Role of the State," *American Political Science Review* 95, 1: 115–30.

Fraga, Luis R., John A. Garcia, Rodney E. Hero, Michael Jones-Correa, Valerie Martinez-Ebers, and Gary M. Segura. 2006. Latino National Survey Project (in progress).

Frymer, Paul. 2005. "Race, Parties, and Democratic Inclusion," in Christina Wolbrecht and Rodney E. Hero, with Peri Arnold and Alvin Tillery (Eds.), *The Politics of Democratic Inclusion*. Philadelphia: Temple University Press, pp. 122–42.

Gilens, Martin. 2003. "How the Poor Became Black," in Sanford F. Schram, Joe Soss, and Richard C. Fording (Eds.), *Race and the Politics of Welfare Reform*. Ann Arbor: University of Michigan Press, pp. 101–30.

Giles, Michael W., and Kaenan Hertz. 1994. "Racial Threat and Partisan Identification," *American Political Science Review* 88: 317–26.

Gimpel, James. 1996. *National Elections and the Autonomy of American State Party Systems*. Pittsburgh: University of Pittsburgh Press.

Gray, Virginia. 1996. "The Socioeconomic and Political Context of States," in Virginia Gray and Herbert Jacob (Eds.), *Politics in the American States*, 6th ed. Washington, DC: Congressional Quarterly Press, pp. 1–34.

Gray, Virginia. 1999. "The Socioeconomic and Political Context of States," in Virginia Gray, Russell L. Hanson, and Herbert Jacob (Eds.), *Politics in the American States*, 7th ed. Washington, DC: Congressional Quarterly Press, pp. 1–31.

Gray, Virginia. 2004. "The Socioeconomic and Political Context of States," in Virginia Gray and Russell L. Hanson (Eds.), *Politics in the American States*, 8th ed. Washington, DC: Congressional Quarterly Press, pp. 1–30.

Guglielmo, Thomas A. 2003. *White upon Arrival: Italians, Race, Color and Power in Chicago, 1890–1945*. New York: Oxford University Press.

Hajnal, Zoltan L., Elisabeth R. Gerber, and Hugh Louch. 2002. "Minorities and Direct Legislation: Evidence from California Ballot Proposition Elections," *Journal of Politics* 64, 1: 154–77.

Hancock, Ange-Marie. 2004. *The Politics of Disgust and the Public Identity of the "Welfare Queen."* New York University Press.

Hanson, Russell L. 1994. "Liberalism and the Course of American Social Welfare Policy," in Lawrence C. Dodd and Calvin Jillson (Eds.), *The Dynamics of American Politics*. Boulder, CO: Westview, pp. 132–59.

Hartz, Louis. 1955. *The Liberal Tradition in America: An Interpretation of American Political Thought Since the Revolution*. New York: Harcourt Brace.

Hawes, Daniel P., Rene R. Rocha, and Kenneth J. Meier. 2006. "Social Capital and Racial Diversity: Evaluating the Determinants of Equity in the American States," Paper presented at the Annual Meeting of the Midwest Political Science Association, Chicago April 20–23.

Hayward, Clarissa Rile. 2003. "The Difference States Make: Democracy, Identity, and the American City," *American Political Science Review* 97, 4: 501–14.

Hero, Rodney E. 1991. "Questions and Approaches in Understanding Latino Politics: The Need for Clarification and Bridging," *National Political Science Review* 3: 153–7.

Hero, Rodney E. 1992. *Latinos and the U.S. Political System: Two-Tiered Pluralism*. Philadelphia: Temple University Press.

Hero, Rodney E. 1998. *Faces of Inequality: Social Diversity in American Politics*. New York: Oxford University Press.

Hero, Rodney E. 2003a. "Social Capital and Racial Inequality in America," *Perspectives on Politics* 1, 1: 113–22.

Hero, Rodney E. 2003b. "Multiple Traditions in American Politics and Racial Policy Inequality," *Political Research Quarterly* 56, 4: 401–8.

Hero, Rodney E., and Robert R. Preuhs. 2006. "Immigration and the Evolving American Welfare State," Working paper, Department of Political Science, University of Notre Dame.

Hero, Rodney E., and Benjamin Radcliff. 2005. *Race, Class and Inequality in the American States* (research project in progress).

Hero, Rodney E., and Caroline J. Tolbert. 1996. "A Racial/Ethnic Diversity Interpretation of Politics and Policy in the States of the U.S.," *American Journal of Political Science* 40, 3: 851–71.

Hero, Rodney E., Caroline J. Tolbert, and Bridgett King. 2006. "Racial Diversity and Barriers to Participation." Paper presented at the Annual Meeting of the Midwest Political Science Association, Chicago, April 20–23.

Hill, Kim Quaile. 1994. *Democracy in the Fifty States*. Lincoln: University of Nebraska Press.

Hill, Kim Q., and Jan Leighley. 1999. "Racial Diversity, Voter Turnout, and Mobilizing Institutions in the United States," *American Politics Quarterly* 27: 275–95.

Hill, Kim Q., and Tetsuya Matsubayashi. 2005. "Civic Engagement and Mass–Elite Policy Agenda Agreement in American Communities," *American Political Science Review* 99, 2: 215–24.

Hochschild, Jennifer L. 1995. *Facing Up to the American Dream: Race, Class and the Soul of the Nation*. Princeton, NJ: Princeton University Press.

Holbrook, Thomas A., and Emily Van Dunk. 1993. "Electoral Competition in the American States," *American Political Science Review* 88, 1: 200–10.

Howard, Christopher. 1999. "The American Welfare State, or States?" *Political Research Quarterly* 52, 2: 421–42.

Jackson, Robert, Robert Brown, and Gerald C. Wright. 1998. "Registration, Turnout, and the Electoral Representativeness of U.S. State Electorates," *American Politics Quarterly* 26, July: 259–87.

Jacobs, Lawrence R., and Theda Skocpol (Eds.). 2005. *Inequality and American Democracy: What We Know and What We Need to Learn*. New York: Russell Sage.

Jacobson, Matthew F. 1998. *Whiteness of a Different Color: European Immigrants and the Alchemy of Race*. Cambridge, MA: Harvard University Press.

Johnson, Martin. 2001. "The Impact of Social Diversity and Racial Attitudes on Social Welfare Policy," *State Politics and Policy Quarterly* 1, 1: 27–49.

Johnson, Martin. 2003. "Racial Context, Public Attitudes, and Welfare Effort in the American States." In Sanford F. Schram, Joe Soss, and Richard C. Fording (Eds.), *Race and the Politics of Welfare Reform*. Ann Arbor: University of Michigan Press, pp. 151–70.

Jones-Correa, Michael. 2000. "The Origins and Diffusion of Racial Restrictive Covenants," *Political Science Quarterly* 115, 4: 541–68.

Katznelson, Ira. 2005. *When Affirmative Action Was White: An Untold Story of Racial Inequality in Twentieth-Century America*. New York: Norton.

Keiser, Lael R., Peter R. Mueser, and Seung-Whan Choi. 2004. "Race, Bureaucratic Discretion and Implementation of Welfare Reform," *American Journal of Political Science* 48, 2: 314–27.

Key, V. O., Jr. 1949. *Southern Politics – In State and Nation*. Knoxville: University of Tennessee Press.

Kinder, Donald R., and Tali Mendelberg. 1995. "Cracks in the American Apartheid: The Political Impact of Prejudice among Desegregated Whites," *Journal of Politics* 57, 2: 402–24.

King, Desmond S. 2000. *Making Americans: Immigration, Race, and the Origins of the Diverse Democracy*. Cambridge, MA: Harvard University Press.

King, Desmond S., and Rogers M. Smith. 2005. "Racial Orders in American Political Development." *American Political Science Review* 99, 1: 75–92.

Klinkner, Philip, with Rogers Smith. 1999. *The Unsteady March: The Rise and Decline of Racial Equality in America*. Chicago: University of Chicago Press.

Knack, Stephen. 2002. "Social Capital and the Quality of Government: Evidence from the States," *American Journal of Political Science* 46, 4: 772–85.

Langer, Laura. 1999. "Measuring Income Distribution across Space and Time in the American States," *Social Science Quarterly* 80, March: 55–67.

Leighley, Jan, and Jonathan Nagler. 1992. "Individual and Systemic Influences on Turnout: Who Votes?" *Journal of Politics* 54, 3: 718–40.

Lewis-Beck, Michael S., and Tom W. Rice. 1992. *Forecasting Elections*. Washington, DC: Congressional Quarterly Press.

Lieberman, Robert. 2003. "Race and the Limits of Solidarity," in Sanford F. Schram, Joe Soss, and Richard C. Fording (Eds.), *Race and the Politics of Welfare Reform*. Ann Arbor: University of Michigan Press, pp. 23–46.

Lieske, Joel. 1993. "Regional Subcultures of the United States," *Journal of Politics* 55, 4: 86–113.

Link, Michael W., and Robert W. Oldendick. 1996. "Social Construction and White Attitude toward Equal Opportunity and Multiculturalism," *Journal of Politics* 58, 1: 149–68.

Lockard, Duane. 1968. *Toward Equal Opportunity: A Study of State and Local Anti-Discrimination Laws*. New York: Macmillan.

Lowi, Theodore H., and Benjamin Ginsberg. 1990. *American Government*. New York: Norton.

Lowndes, Vivien, and David Wilson. 2001. "Social Capital and Local Governance: Exploring the Institutional Design Variable," *Political Studies* 49, 4: 629–45.

Massey, Douglas S., and Nancy Denton. 1993. *American Apartheid: Segregation and the Making of the Underclass*. Cambridge, MA: Harvard University Press.

McDonald, Michael P., and Samuel Popkin. 2001. "The Myth of the Vanishing Voter," *American Political Science Review* 95, 4: 963–74.

Meier, Kenneth, and Joseph Stewart, Jr. 1991. *The Politics of Hispanic Education*. Albany: State University of New York Press.

Meier, Kenneth, Joseph Stewart, Jr., and Robert England. 1989. *Race, Class and Education: The Politics of Second Generation Discrimination*. Madison: University of Wisconsin Press.

Mossberger, Karen, Caroline J. Tolbert, and Mary Stansbury. 2003. *Virtual Inequality: Beyond the Digital Divide*. Washington, DC: Georgetown University Press.

Myrdal, Gunnar. 1944. *An American Dilemma: The Negro Problem and Modern Democracy*. New York: Harper & Brothers.

Nardulli, Peter F. 1990. "Political Subcultures in the American States: An Empirical Examination of Elazar's Formulation," *American Politics Quarterly* 18: 287–315.

Norris, Pippa. 2001. *Digital Divide: Civic Engagement, Information Poverty, and the Internet Worldwide*. Cambridge University Press.

Omi, Michael, and Howard Winant. 1986. *Racial Formation in the United States: From the 1960s to the 1980s*. New York: Routledge & Kegan Paul.

Orr, Marion. 1999. *Black Social Capital: The Politics of School Reform in Baltimore, 1986–1998*. Lawrence: University Press of Kansas.

Orren, Karen, and Stephen Skowronek. 2004. *The Search for American Political Development*. Cambridge University Press.

Pierson, Paul. 1994. *Dismantling the Welfare State? Reagan, Thatcher and the Politics of Retrenchment*. Cambridge University Press.

Pinderhughes, Dianne M. 1987. *Race and Ethnicity in Chicago Politics: A Reexamination of Pluralist Theory*. Urbana: University of Illinois Press.

Piven, Frances Fox, and Richard A. Cloward. 1988. *Why Americans Don't Vote*. New York: Pantheon.

Plotnick, Robert D., and Richard F. Winters. 1985. "A Politico-Economic Theory of Income Redistribution," *American Political Science Review* 79, 2: 458–73.

Putnam, Robert D. 1993. *Making Democracy Work: Civic Traditions in Modern Italy*. Princeton, NJ: Princeton University Press.

Putnam, Robert D. 1995. "Bowling Alone: America's Declining Social Capital," *Journal of Democracy* 6, 1: 65–78.

Putnam, Robert D. 2000. *Bowling Alone: The Collapse and Revival of American Community*. New York: Simon & Schuster.

Putzel, James. 1997. "Accounting for the 'Dark Side' of Social Capital: Reading Robert Putnam on Democracy," *Journal of International Development* 9, 7: 939–49.

Radcliff, Benjamin. 2001. "Politics, Markets, and Life Satisfaction: The Political Economy of Human Happiness," *American Political Science Review* 95, 4: 939–52.

Radcliff, Benjamin, and Martin Saiz. 1995. "Race, Turnout, and Public Policy in the American States," *Political Research Quarterly* 48, 4: 775–94.

Rice, Tom W., and Jan L. Feldman. 1997. "Civic Culture and Democracy from Europe to America," *Journal of Politics* 59, 4: 1143–72.

Rice, Tom W., and Alexander Sumberg. 1997. "Civic Culture and Government Performance in the American States," *Publius: The Journal of Federalism* 27, 1: 99–114.

Rocha, Rene R. 2006. "Racial Threat, Residential Segregation, and the Policy Attitudes of Anglos," Unpublished manuscript, Department of Political Science, Texas A&M University.

Rom, Mark. 1996. "Health and Welfare in the American States: Politics and Policies," in Virginia Gray and Herbert Jacob (Eds.), *Politics in the American States*, 6th ed. Washington, DC: Congressional Quarterly Press, pp. 399–437.

Rom, Mark Carl. 1999. "Transforming State Health and Welfare Programs," in Virginia Gray, Russell Hanson, and Herbert Jacob (Eds.), *Politics in the*

American States, 7th ed. Washington, DC: Congressional Quarterly Press, pp. 349–92.

Rom, Mark Carl. 2004. "Transforming State Health and Welfare Programs," in Virginia Gray and Russell L. Hanson (Eds.), *Politics in the American States*, 7th ed., Washington, DC: Congressional Quarterly Press, pp. 349–92.

Rosenblum, Nancy L. 1998. *Membership and Morals: The Personal Uses of Pluralism in America*. Princeton, NJ: Princeton University Press.

Rosenstone, Steven. J., and John Mark Hansen. 1993. *Mobilization, Participation, and Democracy in America*. New York: Macmillan.

Schattschneider, E. E. 1960. *The Semi-Sovereign People*. Hinsdale, IL: Dryden.

Schmidt, David. 1989. *Citizen Lawmakers: The Ballot Initiative Revolution*. Philadelphia: Temple University Press.

Schmidt, Ronald. 2000. *Language Policy and Identity Politics in the United States*. Philadelphia: Temple University Press.

Schneider, Anne, and Helen Ingram. 1993. "Social Construction of Target Populations: Implications for Public Policy," *American Political Science Review* 87, 2: 334–47.

Schneider, Mark, Paul Teske, Christine Roch, and Melissa Marschall. 1997. "Networks to Nowhere: Segregation and Stratification in Networks of Information about Schools," *American Journal of Political Science* 41, 4: 1201–23.

Sears, David O., John J. Hetts, Jim Sidanius, and Lawrence Bobo. 2000. "Race in American Politics," in David O. Sears, Jim Sidanius, and Lawrence Bobo (Eds.), *Racialized Politics: The Debate about Racism in America*. University of Chicago Press, pp. 1–43.

Sidanius, Jim, Pam Singh, John J. Hetts, and Chris Federico. 2000. "It's Not Affirmative Action, It's the Blacks," in David O. Sears, Jim Sidanius, and Lawrence Bobo (Eds.), *Racialized Politics: The Debate about Racism in America*. University of Chicago Press, pp. 191–235.

Skocpol, Theda. 2003. *Diminished Democracy: From Membership to Management in American Civic Life*. Norman: University of Oklahoma Press.

Skocpol, Theda, Marshall Ganz, and Ziad Munson. 2000. "A Nation of Organizers: The Institutional Origins of Civic Voluntarism in the United States," *American Political Science Review* 94, 3: 527–46.

Skrentny, John D. 2002. *The Minority Rights Revolution*. Cambridge, MA: Belknap.

Smith, Mark. 2001. "The Contingent Effects of Ballot Initiatives and Candidate Races on Turnout," *American Journal of Political Science* 45, 3: 700–6.

Smith, Rogers M. 1993. "Beyond Tocqueville, Myrdal, and Hartz: The Multiple Traditions in America," *American Political Science Review* 87, 3: 549–66.

Smith, Rogers M. 1997. *Civic Ideals: Conflicting Visions of Citizenship in U.S. History*. New Haven, CT: Yale University Press.

Sniderman, Paul M., Gretchen C. Crosby, and William G. Howell. 2000. "The Politics of Race," in David O. Sears, Jim Sidanius, and Lawrence Bobo (Eds.), *Racialized Politics: The Debate about Racism in America*. University of Chicago Press, pp. 236–79.

Soss, Joe, Laura Langbein, and A. Metelko. 2003. "Why Do White Americans Support the Death Penalty?" *Journal of Politics* 65, 2: 397–421.

Soss, Joe, Sanford F. Schram, Thomas P. Varanian, and Erin O'Brien. 2001. "Setting the Terms of Relief: Explaining State Policy Choices in the Devolution Revolution," *American Journal of Political Science* 45, 2: 378–95.

Stevens, Jacqueline. 1995. "Beyond Tocqueville, Please" *American Political Science Review* 89, 4: 987–95.

Stolle, Dietlind, and Marc Hooghe. 2005. "Inaccurate, Exceptional, One-Sided or Irrelevant? The Debate about the Alleged Decline of Social Capital and Civic Engagement in Western Societies," *British Journal of Political Science* 35, 1: 149–67.

Stone, Clarence. 1980. "Systemic Power in Community Decision Making: A Restatement of Stratification Theory," *American Political Science Review* 74, 4: 978–90.

Stone, Clarence N. 1989. *Regime Politics: Governing Atlanta, 1946–1988*. Lawrence: University Press of Kansas.

Stone, Clarence N., Jeffrey R. Henig, Bryan D. Jones, and Carol Pierannunzi. 2001. *Building Civic Capacity: The Politics of Reforming Urban Schools*. Lawrence: University Press of Kansas.

Strolovitch, Dara. 2007. *Affirmative Advocacy: Marginilization, Representation, and Interest Group Politics*. University of Chicago Press.

Tarrow, Sidney. 1996. "Making Social Science Work across Space and Time: A Critical Reflection on Robert Putnam's *Making Democracy Work*," *American Political Science Review* 90, 2: 389–97.

Theiss-Morse, Elizabeth, and John R. Hibbing. 2005. "Citizenships and Civic Engagement," *Annual Review of Political Science* 8, June: 227–49.

Thompson, Michael, Richard Ellis, and Aaron Wildavsky. 1990. *Cultural Theory*. Boulder, Co: Westview.

Tocqueville, Alexis de 1958 [1835]. *Democracy in America* (Richard D. Heffner, Ed.). New York: New American Library.

Tolbert, Caroline J. 2005. "The Ballot Measure/Citizen Interest Link: Information, Engagement and Participation," Paper presented at the Impact of Direct Democracy Conference, University of California, Irvine (January).

Tolbert, Caroline J., and John Grummel. 2003. "White Voter Support for California's Proposition 209: Revisiting the Racial Threat Hypothesis," *State Politics and Policy Quarterly* 3, 2: 183–202.

Tolbert, Caroline J., John Grummel, and Daniel Smith. 2001. "The Effects of Ballot Initiatives on Voter Turnout in the United State," *American Politics Research* 29, 6: 625–48.

Tolbert, Caroline J., and Rodney E. Hero. 1996. "Race/Ethnicity and Direct Democracy: An Analysis of California's Illegal Immigration Initiative," *Journal of Politics* 58, 3: 806–18.

Tolbert, Caroline J., and Ramona McNeal. 2003. "Unraveling the Effects of the Internet on Political Participation," *Political Research Quarterly* 56, 2: 175–85.

Tolbert, Caroline J., Ramona McNeal, and Daniel Smith. 2003. "Enhancing Civic Engagement: The Effects of Direct Democracy on Political Participation and Knowledge," *State Politics and Policy Quarterly* 3, 1: 23–41.

Tolbert, Caroline J., and Daniel A. Smith. 2005. "The Educative Effects of Ballot Initiatives on Voter Turnout," *American Political Research* 33, 2: 283–309.

Tolbert, Caroline J., and Gertrude Steuernagel. 2001. "Women Lawmakers, State Mandates and Women's Health," *Women and Politics* 22, 2: 1–39.

Verba, Sidney, and Norman H. Nie. 1972. *Participation in America*. New York: Harper & Row.

Verba, Sidney, Kay L. Schlozman, and Henry E. Brady. 1995. *Voice and Equality: Civic Voluntarism in American Politics*. Cambridge, MA: Harvard University Press.

Ward, Deborah E. 2005. *The White Welfare State: The Racialization of U.S. Welfare Policy*. Ann Arbor: University of Michigan Press.

Winters, Richard F. 1999. "The Politics of Taxing and Spending," in Virginia Gray and Russell Hanson (Eds.), *Politics in the American States*, 7th ed. Washington, DC: Congressional Quarterly Press, pp. 304–48.

Wolbrecht, Christina. 2005. "Mediating Institutions," in Christina Wolbrecht and Rodney E. Hero, with Peri Arnold and Alvin Tillery (Eds.), *The Politics of Democratic Inclusion*. Philadelphia: Temple University Press, pp. 103–7.

Wolfinger, Raymond, and Steven J. Rosenstone. 1980. *Who Votes?* New Haven, CT: Yale University Press.

Index